I was captivated by Michael's won[...]
storytelling. The Bible characters[...]
through the hopes, heartaches, difficulties and dreams that, in God's hands, add that special *je ne sais quoi* to the seasons of our lives. Each reflection was so vivid I couldn't wait to read the next.
Michele Guinness, writer and speaker

This book comes as a welcome reminder that there really is more than one season. The unpredictability of life may mean that we find ourselves in seasons in which the focus of activity is internal rather than external, or preparatory rather than productive. This very practical book serves as a wise and gracious toolkit for anyone in any season. Like the seasons themselves, it is a gift for our souls.
Roger Morris, Bishop of Colchester

The Bible Reading Fellowship
15 The Chambers, Vineyard
Abingdon OX14 3FE
brf.org.uk

The Bible Reading Fellowship (BRF) is a Registered Charity (233280)

ISBN 978 0 85746 540 5
First published 2017
10 9 8 7 6 5 4 3 2 1 0
All rights reserved

Text © Michael Mitton 2017
This edition © The Bible Reading Fellowship 2017
Cover image © MHJ/DigitalVision Vectors/Getty Images
Inside illustrations by Rebecca J Hall

Acknowledgements
Scripture quotations from The New Revised Standard Version of the Bible, Anglicised
edition, copyright © 1989, 1995 by the Division of Christian Education of the National
Council of the Churches of Christ in the United States of America. Used by permission.
All rights reserved.

Every effort has been made to trace and contact copyright owners for material used
in this resource. We apologise for any inadvertent omissions or errors, and would
ask those concerned to contact us so that full acknowledgement can be made in
the future.

A catalogue record for this book is available from the British Library

Printed and bound by CPI Group (UK) Ltd, Croydon CR0 4YY

SEASONED BY SEASONS

Flourishing in life's experiences

MICHAEL MITTON

To Eric, Russ, John, Steve and Nick
With such heartfelt gratitude for your extraordinary companionship.
Together we have laughed, loved, wined, wept, prayed and praised
our way through every season.

CONTENTS

SPRING: the season of birthing

SUMMER: the season of flourishing

INTRODUCTION

Towards the end of Shakespeare's *The Merchant of Venice*, the heroine of the play, Portia, is taking an evening walk with her waiting maid, Nerissa. They hear some music and notice its particular quality when heard in the night-time. Then Portia, whom we know by this stage of the play to be someone of impressive wisdom and insight, delivers one of her beautiful speeches:

> *The crow doth sing as sweetly as the lark*
> *When neither is attended; and, I think,*
> *The nightingale, if she should sing by day,*
> *When every goose is cackling, would be thought*
> *No better a musician than the wren.*
> *How many things by season season'd are*
> *To their right praise and true perfection!*[1]

Portia is noticing that things are at their best when in the right place and time. She says that there is something exquisite about the sound of a nightingale singing away in the dark hours of the night. But to hear it among the cacophony of cackling geese in broad daylight would make it much less special. Though some may fear the dark as inhospitable and full of threats, it is the night that is the welcome host for this beautiful songbird. Night and day, light and dark all have their purposes.

'For everything there is a season,'[2] says that engaging writer of the book of Ecclesiastes, who observes that life has to go through many different seasons, with each season having value and virtue. And Shakespeare, through Portia, ponders how many things in life are seasoned by the various seasons we find ourselves in. I don't know enough about Shakespeare to know quite how he was using the word 'season' there. Was it to do with the seasoning of adding flavour? Or was it about the way we talk about wood being seasoned when it has been allowed to dry out and has become tough and resilient? In my experience, both are true when it comes to the passage of the soul that passes through many seasons. These seasons of life through which we journey can indeed act like seasoning – we pick up sprinklings of wisdom and insight and are all the richer for it. And there are many experiences of life that produce a hardiness that equips us well for the onward journey.

For those of us who live well clear of the equator, the seasons are well defined. In early Celtic Britain, they were marked out not so much by weather as by daylight. Thus, the first of May marked the first day of summer – the season of three months in the middle of which the sun was at its highest. The first of November marked the start of the winter trimester, during the middle of which the sun was at its lowest. In between these were the seasons of spring and autumn, and in the middle of those seasons fell the equinox, those two days of the year when the measures of light and dark are the same.

In many respects, the seasons through which our souls travel are very much influenced by light. In this case, not so much literal daylight (though many of us are influenced in our souls by the presence and absence of daylight), but more the kind of light that John's Gospel speaks about. Here was a writer who loved playing with the concept of light, and the work he so carefully crafted about the life and teaching of Jesus is full of references to a light that enlightens the soul. Listen to the first few words of his book where he introduces us to Jesus, whom at this stage of his book he calls 'the Word':

> What has come into being in him was life, and the life was the light of all people. The light shines in the darkness, and the darkness did not overcome it. There was a man sent from God, whose name was John. He came as a witness to testify to the

light, so that all might believe through him. He himself was
not the light, but he came to testify to the light. The true light,
which enlightens everyone, was coming into the world.

JOHN 1:3–9

After such a blazing start to his Gospel, you might think all that
follows will be high-summer daylight. But this is far from the
case. Yes, there certainly are the bright days of glorious healings,
miraculous feedings of thousands of people, the poor hearing great
news and the abusive powers being challenged. But you also have
Nicodemus coming by night[3] because he is terrified by the thought
of what his fellow religious leaders might think of him. When you
read his story, you can see his furrowed brow and glancing eyes,
and hear his searching questions and you can't help but feel the
longings in the hidden recesses of his heart. And, of course, as you
move on in this book, the shadows lengthen across the life of Jesus,
so much so that one terrible afternoon the sun turns its face away
from this earth, leaving deep darkness over the mount where the
limp, lifeless body of Jesus hangs. But the story does not end there,
because two days after these fearful events John gets going again
with another dark and light story: 'Early on the first day of the week,
while it was still dark...'[4] In this severe dark night of the soul, Mary
Magdalene, one of the people who loved Jesus most, fumbles her
way to the tomb, only to discover that a greater light than she ever
could have imagined has broken into the world in the form of her
radiant resurrected Messiah.

Such toing and froing of light and dark is so typical of our lives. I find
it doesn't take much to send either light or dark across my path. I can
be having a day full of brightness, but then one piece of bad news
causes the sun to go in and the thunderclouds roll over to darken
my land. Equally, I have also known times when I thought the path
ahead looked fairly gloomy, only to find unexpected shafts of light
leading me on, not only keeping me from stumbling, but enabling
me to be delighted by surprise discoveries.

I find it so encouraging to thumb my way through my Bible and discover that it is full of very human stories of people who experienced just the same thing. I find in these ancient scriptures varying stories of spring, summer, autumn and winter. Whether it is in the stories themselves, or the reflections of the writer, I have found guides here to help me make the most of every season.

The chapters that follow will take us through the different seasons and I shall pick up some themes that seem particularly suited to each season. The allocations of subjects to seasons is not a precise science, so you might reckon, for example, that a reading set for winter might be better placed in autumn. You are free to do your own editing. This is a book that you can start at the beginning and work your way through, or you may prefer just to dip into a chapter or life experience that seems particularly relevant. Each reading will have a question for reflection and a prayer to help connect the Bible story with your story.

We have to recognise that, in our own journey of the soul, the seasons do not necessarily follow the order that we see in the outer world. In that world, spring always follows winter, and autumn always follows summer. But in the seasons of the soul, we can experience a beautiful springtime, but then a sudden loss can throw us into an autumn. One season may last several months, and another a few days. There is really no telling which season is coming next. But the Bible stories in this book tell us that we are given what we need to face whichever season comes our way.

Traditionally, the Bible has been a guidebook for Christians, but increasingly I am finding that people of no particular religious persuasion are intrigued by the stories and teachings of the Bible. They recognise that it never was designed for the exclusive use of religious people. Yes, there are parts (such as some of Paul's teaching in his letters) that are directed to church people to help them with specific churchy issues, but so much of the Bible is written to all people who are simply trying to make sense of this precious life we have been given. The book of Proverbs, for example, is full of wisdom that is as relevant to our world today as it was to the world for which it was originally written. The great stories of Noah, Joseph, Ruth and Mary are still brimful of imaginative life and drama and succeed in fascinating us. All four of the Gospel stories were written for people outside the church to tell the world about the story of this carpenter's son from Nazareth who turned out to be much more than a carpenter's son.

Every story recorded in the Bible is inevitably only a small snapshot of the event that happened. We are meant to use our imaginations to bring it to life, and in the readings that follow I have recorded what I 'see' in these life events. Those familiar with Ignatian spirituality will know the value of using the gift of imagination. I hope what I have written will spark your imagination, to help you discover the treasures of each story. Hopefully, too, it will encourage you to do your own imaginative journey with these special stories.

It never ceases to amaze me how I can visit a passage of the Bible which I may have read countless times, and yet find in it a new discovery that becomes a source of deep life for me. How you explain this, I don't know. 'All Scripture is inspired by God,'[5] wrote Paul to his friend Timothy, and it is certainly my experience that very often as I settle myself into a passage from the Bible, something about it comes alive and I become aware of the presence of God as I inhale it into my soul.

'How many things by season season'd are to their right praise and true perfection?' wonders Portia. This seasoning leads to praise and perfection. The 'praise', as I understand it, is that response of gratitude that comes from the discovery that life can thrive in any season. The 'perfection' I think is not so much to do with a goody-goody perfection, but rather in the sense of an artist seeking to perfect her craft – that intention to work at something until it becomes all that it can be. This is the gift of all seasons – each can work on our souls to enable us to become more than we ever thought possible. May our exploration of these passages of ancient writing do just that.

> And God said, 'Let there be lights in the dome of the sky to separate the day from the night; and let them be for signs and for seasons and for days and years, and let them be lights in the dome of the sky to give light upon the earth.' And it was so.
> GENESIS 1:14–15

AUTUMN

The season of
creating space

INTRODUCTION

In the early Celtic calendar, autumn began on 1 August, and they called this season *Lammas*, an Anglo-Saxon word derived from *hlaf-mas*, meaning 'the mass loaf'. This was the day when you brought to church a loaf made from the fresh harvest of the new grain crop. During this season, most of the produce from the land would ripen and be harvested. Autumn is a season of fruitfulness, but also, as it progresses, it is a time where the long days of summer get noticeably shorter, the deciduous trees turn colour and release their leaves to the ground.

Shelley begins one of his odes with,

> *I stood within the city disinterred*
> *And heard the autumnal leaves, like light footfalls*
> *of spirits passing through the streets*[6]

Autumn has that feeling of life being let go, as spirits are released from the body at death. There is a theme of dying in the autumn – much in nature appears to die off and lose the vigorous life of summer. The season of autumn ends with Halloween, the festival that traditionally heralds All Saints Day, the day of remembering those who have died. And yet, despite this theme of dying and loss, autumn can be one of the most beautiful and striking of the seasons, especially where such trees as maples and aspens flare up in rich golds and crimsons.

Autumn therefore is a curious mix of celebration and loss. The losses are considerable: the loss of warmth, rich foliage, colourful flowers, crop-filled fields and of course the light, which is rapidly retreating by the time we get to the autumn equinox. But nature also tells us that all this letting go is for a reason. All the harvest produce is made up of what the earth has released for us. It is perhaps the deciduous trees that are most articulate about one of the great messages of autumn. Watch those fluttering leaves pile up beneath the great ashes, oaks, chestnuts and sycamores. Little by little, they change and become humus. That humus sinks down, and becomes the earth around those slender roots that sustains the tree for the next season of life.

In the Bible, we discover many stories to do with the great range of losses suffered by humankind. What I notice in them is that when people bring these experiences into a perspective of faith in God, they discover that the willingness to let go and grieve creates space for new possibilities. This kind of grieving creates space for new vision. They begin to see things in a new light. It was the prophet Isaiah who brought this message from God to a group of people who had experienced severe losses:

> Do not remember the former things,
>   or consider the things of old.
> I am about to do a new thing;
>   now it springs forth, do you not perceive it?
> ISAIAH 43:18–19[7]

The biblical scholar Walter Brueggemann wrote 'only grief permits newness'.[8] If he is right, then if we want springtime newness in our souls, we must learn to grieve well. The autumns that come our way nearly always involve some kind of grieving, and when this is well done then space is created for new possibilities.

FEAR – SPACE FOR NEW CONFIDENCE

On that day, when evening had come, [Jesus] said to [his disciples], 'Let us go across to the other side.' And leaving the crowd behind, they took him with them in the boat, just as he was. Other boats were with him. A great gale arose, and the waves beat into the boat, so that the boat was already being swamped. But he was in the stern, asleep on the cushion; and they woke him up and said to him, 'Teacher, do you not care that we are perishing?' He woke up and rebuked the wind, and said to the sea, 'Peace! Be still!' Then the wind ceased, and there was a dead calm. He said to them, 'Why are you afraid? Have you still no faith?' And they were filled with great awe and said to one another, 'Who then is this, that even the wind and the sea obey him?'

MARK 4:35–41 (see also MARK 1:14–20)

The story of Jesus asleep in the storm-tossed boat is well known. It has been trawled by many a preacher, who, in their sermons, release their catch of good points to their congregations who leave church knowing they must not be anxious or afraid, and must trust Jesus who calms every storm of life. And yet, when they get home, it will take only a phone call to dislodge the message of the sermon, and once again they are nervously grasping the side of a rocking boat wondering whether their God really will come to their rescue, or whether he might as well be a sleeping deity in the midst of a human storm.

To help me envisage this story, I find it easier to home in on one of the disciples, so I am going to think about how this event might have been for Andrew. He is Peter's brother and we know he is a fisherman and therefore he is familiar with this world of boats, lakes and storms. He is quite happy to launch out into the lake as night falls. In the old days, when he worked this lake for fish, he was often out in the hours of darkness. Perhaps, on this occasion, they are using his boat. So there he is back in his familiar world, shipping Jesus and his friends to the other side of the lake. But then it happens. He knows the signs – that familiar disturbance of air that will all too quickly become a squall, tossing the boat on the heaving lake. Heavy raindrops spatter into the wooden craft. His friends pull their thick robes over themselves for shelter. It is now so dark that it is hard to make out who's who on the boat. Andrew has steered his boat through many a storm before now, but this looks like being a mean one, and, as luck would have it, they are as far from shore as is possible on this great lake. But he is in charge of this boat, and he must get them to land as fast as he can.

Yet, try as he might, Andrew cannot get control of his boat, and he begins to realise that he is losing the battle against this storm. Peter is shouting something at him and others are screaming advice. In the storm-force wind, the raindrops feel sharp and fierce even on his rugged face. He has always been a strong and courageous man, but he feels such courage drain from him in the face of this gale.

He feels fear in his guts. And he has every right to be afraid; his life is in real danger. He passes a rope to Peter and struggles his way to the stern past the others, who are all shouting things now. Jesus has done some pretty impressive things in recent days; surely he can help? But when he gets to the stern of the boat, he is astonished to find Jesus curled up and fast asleep on the fishing nets! The boat is tossing around like an untamed donkey. Water is drenching Jesus, but even that doesn't wake him. Andrew clambers closer and grasps his arm. Ever since he had chosen to follow this Jesus of Nazareth, the world had become such a safe place for him. This rabbi demonstrated again and again how much he cared for people. Andrew was getting to the point where he really did believe that he truly was the Son of God, the Messiah for whom his people had longed with such a desperate and deep yearning. But what use was it having the Son of God in your boat if all he could do was sleep when you really needed him? Surely you should not have to rouse God from his slumbers?

In desperation, Andrew shakes Jesus by the shoulders and screams at him to wake up. It's difficult to see his face in this thick darkness and if he is going to say anything it will be nigh impossible to hear him above the roar of the storm. 'Teacher, don't you care about us?' Andrew yells accusingly. Jesus eventually wakes and somehow or other he manages to stand up on this wildly pitching boat and gazes out to sea, unperturbed by the rain slashing at his face. Andrew is clinging to the straining mast and looks beseechingly at Jesus. Then he hears an angry cry from his master – Jesus is shouting not at those in the boat but at the very storm itself. He is commanding it to stop! Before Andrew has a chance to think about how ridiculous a notion this is, the storm abruptly dies. The wind and rain cease from their violence, and waves that only moments before were as mountains become a still plain. The boat calms and the only sound is the gentle water lapping against its wooden frame. A thin band of light appears on the horizon as Jesus turns and looks at Andrew and says, not with accusation but with genuine curiosity, 'Why are you so afraid? Have you still no faith?' It is a question that is as disturbing as the storm.

Thankfully, most of us do not have to face the kind of terror that Andrew faced, but nonetheless we all know the power of fear. Anxiety is a close relative of fear and regularly stalks the human heart, robbing it of its peace. Even if we have never been at sea in a storm, we can relate to this well-known story. Every journey of faith will have its times of real testing, where to all intents and purposes it feels like God is fast asleep and we are left on our own to face the buffeting storms of life that make us so anxious and afraid. If we were able to talk to Andrew today, I guess he would look at us with real understanding and sympathy. And then he might smile and say, 'Well, in the end he *did* wake up. The calming of the storm was breath taking. It was almost terrifying to see his power. But do you know what I remember most? It was the look on his face when he asked, "Have you still no faith?" It was the love that shifted our fear that night, not the power. It beckoned something from us.'

He might well advise us that the healing of our fears is not wrought by grabbing God's attention so he can sort out the storms that assail us. It is about discovering that his restful presence is in every storm-tossed moment of our lives. We and the world we inhabit may feel like they are in frightening turmoil at times. But there is one who is greater than the storm, whose peace is unmoved by the turbulence and terrors of this world. Confidence grows in us when we catch sight of the watery eyes of love that beckon forth from our own hearts a voice of faith that lets the storm know, in no uncertain terms, just who is in charge.

Reflection

What storm of life is making you anxious today? Try breathing deeply and then imagine you are drawing the peace of Christ into that place of anxiety. Then try telling that storm just who is in charge!

Prayer

When the storms of fear rise and threaten to swamp me, let me feel your peace, O my Saviour, and from that stillness let faith rise through the storm.

INFIRMITY - SPACE FOR WHOLENESS

David asked, 'Is there still anyone left of the house of Saul to whom I may show kindness for Jonathan's sake?' Now there was a servant of the house of Saul whose name was Ziba, and he was summoned to David. The king said to him... 'Is there anyone remaining of the house of Saul to whom I may show the kindness of God?' Ziba said to the king, 'There remains a son of Jonathan; he is crippled in his feet...' Mephibosheth son of Jonathan son of Saul came to David, and fell on his face and did obeisance. David said, 'Mephibosheth!' He answered, 'I am your servant.' David said to him, 'Do not be afraid, for I will show you kindness for the sake of your father Jonathan; I will restore to you all the land of your grandfather Saul, and you yourself shall eat at my table always.' He did obeisance and said, 'What is your servant, that you should look upon a dead dog such as I am?'

Then the king summoned Saul's servant Ziba, and said to him, 'All that belonged to Saul and to all his house I have given to your master's grandson... Mephibosheth shall always eat at my table...' Mephibosheth ate at David's table, like one of the king's sons.

2 SAMUEL 9:1–11 (abridged) (see also 2 SAMUEL 4:1–4; 2 SAMUEL 9:12–13)

There are a large number of stories in the Bible where ill people are miraculously and wonderfully healed through a touch from God. I have witnessed healings of this sort myself, and I have been left speechless with delight seeing someone freed from the illness that had beset them. Such experiences belong in the high summer of joy and thanksgiving. But there is an autumn season in the human journey that is brought about by a loss of health that finds no immediate cure. This may be a short-term illness or injury, or it might be a much longer-term problem where we are assailed by an illness such as chronic fatigue, or where an illness or accident leaves us with a disability. Experiences of loss of physical, mental or spiritual health can be very disorientating and, in the journey of Christian faith where there are testimonies of miraculous cures, it can be profoundly confusing.

Our guide for today is someone who is found at the edge of the great David stories. He was the kind of person who would have been astonished to turn up in anyone's storybook, let alone that of the greatest king of Israel. David followed on after Saul, the first king of Israel, and the two had a rather troubled relationship. But David was devoted to Saul's son Jonathan. Mephibosheth was Jonathan's son, but when he was only five years old, he lost his father and grandfather in a great battle. As a close relative of royalty, he was suddenly in a very vulnerable position, so his nurse attempted to rush him to safety. As if the bereavement was not bad enough, Mephibosheth then suffered further as his nurse managed to drop him in her panic and he suffered an injury to his legs that left him disabled. Our reading today also suggests that, as he grew up, Mephibosheth suffered from a fairly poor self-image. Many in that culture were not kind to people with disabilities. So he grew up in hiding until the day King David discovered he was alive, and called him to his palace.

We only have snippets of information about Mephibosheth, so we have to use our imaginations to make up what is missing. He is nervous as he travels to the palace of the great king. He looks at his misshapen feet that were so disastrously damaged in that fall. He still feels the ache of bereavement as he thinks back on the father he lost at such a young age. He fears the taunts of those who mock him for his infirmity. His illness feels like a curse from God. So how will this God-appointed king treat him? Will he be in for further humiliation? Or worse?

He is ushered into the palace and there is the great king. He does his best to bow down, and one of his crutches clatters to the floor. Without it he fears falling, but then he feels the firm grip of the king on his elbow helping him up. The king addresses him not in words of formality, but of extraordinary tenderness: 'Do not be afraid.' He has known fear since the day he had to flee his home and nursed his aching feet in a place of hiding. But now he feels old fears slipping from him as the king walks him carefully to a table where a sumptuous meal is spread. He had heard of David's great love for his father, and now he feels that love overflowing to himself. Over the meal, this great but tender king restores to him lands and property that were lost after the fatal battle. In a very short space of time, his life has been completely turned around.

So Mephibosheth makes his home in the palace of the king. There is no sudden, miraculous cure to his disability. He will still have his days of hurting feet and a hurting heart as he hears stories of his father and feels the pain of loss. But something inwardly has been healed. His wounds and losses have found a place in this world where they can be held, and it is in the palace of the king.

Preachers and theologians have often made links between David and Jesus. Indeed, Jesus was often called 'Son of David'.[9] Jesus was extraordinarily welcoming to people of ill health in a society that was actually rather critical of them. In Jesus' day, those with illnesses such as leprosy were considered 'unclean' by the religious leaders. Rather than avoiding those pronounced 'unclean', Jesus did quite the opposite, and reached out and touched them. Jesus is the David that welcomes the likes of Mephibosheth to his table. Reading the snippets of story we have from his life, Mephibosheth seems to have found a way of flourishing in that palace, which was rooted in his dwelling in a place of true belonging.

We may have entered a season where we feel a new vulnerability due to our loss of health. We may worry about how people will view or treat us. We may be grieving the loss of the good health we once enjoyed. We may be anxious for our future. But what this engaging story of David and Mephibosheth tells us is that there is always a welcome for us at the table of the King. In reading the Gospel stories, we discover a Son of God who embraced all, no matter what their level of health. His is the table to which we can limp with confidence. It may be that in time we do discover the cure for which we so long. But until such a moment, we can spend time at the royal table and discover what it is to be truly whole in this world.

Reflection

What does it mean to you to be welcomed at the royal table?

Prayer

Lord, when my strength and health fail, lead me to your table that I may find true wholeness.

REJECTION – SPACE FOR TRUE VALUE

Now Sarai, Abram's wife, bore him no children. She had an Egyptian slave-girl whose name was Hagar, and Sarai said to Abram, 'You see that the Lord has prevented me from bearing children; go in to my slave-girl; it may be that I shall obtain children by her.' And Abram listened to the voice of Sarai. So, after Abram had lived for ten years in the land of Canaan, Sarai, Abram's wife, took Hagar the Egyptian, her slave-girl, and gave her to her husband Abram as a wife. He went in to Hagar, and she conceived; and when she saw that she had conceived, she looked with contempt on her mistress. Then Sarai said to Abram, 'May the wrong done to me be on you! I gave my slave-girl to your embrace, and when she saw that she had conceived, she looked on me with contempt. May the Lord judge between you and me!' But Abram said to Sarai, 'Your slave-girl is in your power; do to her as you please.' Then Sarai dealt harshly with her, and she ran away from her.

The angel of the Lord found her by a spring of water in the wilderness, the spring on the way to Shur. And he said, 'Hagar, slave-girl of Sarai, where have you come from and where are you going?'

GENESIS 16:1–8 (see also all of GENESIS 16; GENESIS 21:9–19)

Abraham and Sarah (known by their earlier names of Abram and Sarai in this story) are traditionally regarded as tremendous examples of faith. They certainly had faith in bucketfuls and are inspiring and impressive. But the writers of these great stories do not hide from us the fact that they also had their weak points, and one of their major weak points was their handling of the slave girl, Hagar.

Hagar should be the patron saint of those who suffer the indignity and pain of rejection. For a start, she was a slave, so she had no rights in her life of servitude. Abraham and Sarah had been in Egypt and presumably acquired her there. So she finds herself taken from her family, her homeland and her freedom, and she has to learn a new language and adapt to an unfamiliar culture as she travels with these two rather bewildering elderly people who tell her they are on a God-inspired journey to a promised land.

Presumably, at first she has to do all the menial tasks expected from a slave, but then one day she is presented with a command that must have taken her aback. She was to become a surrogate mother for her owners. She has no say in the matter – she has to sleep with her master, and sure enough she does conceive and finds herself carrying a child. Despite the enslaved conditions that led to this event, you get the feeling that she is delighted at the chance to have a child. But then things turn bad again for Hagar, for Sarah is filled with jealousy and makes life hard for her, so much so that she has to flee.

So let's pause at this pivotal moment in her life story and imagine how this might have been for Hagar. She is a single, pregnant slave, who has suffered severe humiliation and rejection and knows that all will despise her. So we see her in the wilderness, far from all that makes for warmth and safety in this world. She finds a spring of water bubbling out of the arid earth, and there she kneels in the mud, scooping water into her dry mouth, longing for a deeper water to heal and refresh her soul. But in her belly she feels the stirrings of the one life that she can love and who will love her. She washes her tired face in the cool water and it glistens in the sunlight. Then she hears a voice. All voices revile her, and surely this one will be no different. And yet it is. And it asks her two most searching life questions: 'Where have you come from?' and 'Where are you going?'

'I'm on the run,' says Hagar to this unknown figure standing near her, whom she realises is more than human. She steadies herself against a rock and wipes her eyes to check she is not seeing things. The babe in her womb shifts position as the creature tells her to return to her mistress – the last thing she wants to do. But something about this creature awakens confidence in her. There is more to the message, including the words, 'for the Lord has given heed to your affliction' (v. 11). This is the turning point for Hagar. The whole world might be out to get her, but God isn't. To know this is transformative. And so she stands there, water still falling from her dark Egyptian hair. She is no longer a runaway slave; she is a woman who has caught the attention of God Almighty. She is suddenly so empowered, she does something no one else does in the Bible: she gives God a name (v. 13). She realises this visitor in the desert is none other than a manifestation of God. Despite being a slave, she doesn't cower or flinch in his presence. She looks him in the eye. He has named her son, Ishmael, which means 'God hears'. In turn she names God 'El-roi', which means 'God sees'. He has seen the story of her life, and seen the longings of her heart. He does not see her as a slave, but as a human with dignity. Far from rejecting her, he treats her with great tenderness.

So Hagar returns and gives birth to Ishmael. A few years later (Genesis 21), she is on the run again and once more finds herself in a wilderness that is so severe that she and her son nearly die. But the writer touchingly writes, 'God heard the boy's cry' (vv. 17–18). Yes, this is the God who sees and hears. Once again Hagar is restored in a desperate wilderness by an encounter with God.

In the story of Hagar, we are taken into the terrible human crime of slavery – that appalling capacity in the human heart to use other humans for their own ends. Slaves know the severe pains of human rejection. Most of us have experienced the hurt of rejection, and we know our capacity to respond with anger and bitterness. Hagar shows us another path – in her wilderness of extreme rejection, she twice discovered a presence with her of a God who did not join in with the cruel, judgemental and dismissive voices. He came to her as one who hears and sees. And he was one who imparted such value on Hagar that she was allowed to do one thing that even the likes of Moses and Jacob could not do: she was allowed to give God a name.

Reflection.

How do you feel about the God who sees and hears you? What name would you give him?

Prayer

In the harsh wilderness of rejection, help me to discover you, O Lord, for you see my life and hear my story.

VULNERABILITY – SPACE FOR TRUE SAFETY

Now there was a woman who had been suffering from haemorrhages for twelve years; and though she had spent all she had on physicians, no one could cure her. She came up behind [Jesus] and touched the fringe of his clothes, and immediately her haemorrhage stopped. Then Jesus asked, 'Who touched me?' When all denied it, Peter said, 'Master, the crowds surround you and press in on you.' But Jesus said, 'Someone touched me; for I noticed that power had gone out from me.' When the woman saw that she could not remain hidden, she came trembling; and falling down before him, she declared in the presence of all the people why she had touched him, and how she had been immediately healed. He said to her, 'Daughter, your faith has made you well; go in peace.'

LUKE 8:43–48 (see also LUKE 8:40–56)

This is a story within a story, and both stories find people in profound states of vulnerability. The 'outer' story, in the surrounding verses in this chapter, is about a man who is beside himself with anxiety because his twelve-year-old daughter is dangerously ill. Those who have been parents in this world know how vulnerable life feels when their child is in any kind of danger. The 'inner' story involves a woman who would have preferred to have been found at the back of a crowd rather than as the centre of attention. She faces the vulnerability of a long-term illness that constantly drains the life from her. Not only does she have to battle with the illness but, according to the law, she was 'unclean'.[10] Her religion had taught her that she was defiled and therefore could not draw close to God. She also had to keep clear of contact with people because they would be defiled if she touched them. A lonelier existence is hard to imagine. For twelve years this wretched illness had refused to budge from her life; for twelve years she lived with the assumption that, in her condition, any self-respecting God would also keep well clear and have nothing to do with her.

There comes a day, however, when a rabbi with a reputation heads into town. She has heard talk of this rabbi called Jesus, and he seems different to the others. For a start, he is apparently a miracle-worker and it now feels that only a miracle will rescue her from her plight. A neighbour tells her that an important man called Jairus, who runs the synagogue, has called for this rabbi to help his little girl who is desperately sick. The woman realises that if Jesus is heading for Jairus' home, then he'll come right past her house. She would love to take even a brief look at him. She nervously stands on the doorstep, brushing her skirts, making herself look as respectable and healthy as she can. Other neighbours look at her with their well-worn looks of disapproval.

Noise builds up at the end of the street, and there he is, rounding the corner. The distinguished-looking ruler is gripping him by the elbow and guiding him down the street, pushing people out of their way in his haste. A barking dog is zigzagging just ahead of them. Everyone is animated apart from Jesus, who looks curiously calm, even a little detached from the hubbub around him. She grips her hands together tightly and dares to wonder. Could the passing presence of this miracle-worker free her from her illness? But she must not let him see her. She must not bring shame upon him. She hates the thought of the crowd looking at her. He is on such an important errand. The little girl's plight is far more serious than hers. She must stay where she is. People like her are just a nuisance. And yet, and yet... The little dog barks its way past her threshold, and there he is right in front of her – this man they are all talking about. She pretends to drop something, stoops down and briefly grasps the hem of his garment as he passes.

In that moment, something like a fire courses its way from her hand right through her body until it shoots through her feet. She is knocked back and slumps somewhat concussed in her doorway. People crush past her – she is unable to stop herself from touching them. She worries about how many she has made unclean. But then the crowd stops. Something has happened at the front. She pulls herself up – my, she feels so much stronger. But even standing on tiptoe she can't see what's going on. The crowd is going quiet and she only hears one voice, repeating the same question: 'Who touched me?' It is the voice of the rabbi, and she instinctively knows he is looking for her, and she knows he will not move on until she owns up. She wants to hide, and yet she must own up, for the sake of the little girl. Jesus must get moving again.

She raises her hand and feels horribly exposed and found out. Some of those who know her start tut-tutting, and pull themselves back so as to make no contact with her. But Jesus makes his way towards her and, as if he has all the time in the world, pauses and looks at her intently. For the rest of her days she attempted to tell people about these few moments, but she never found words to describe the expression on his face, the tone of his voice and the touch of his hand on her arm. She forgot what he said, apart from one word: 'daughter'. He was God in human form – she knew it. She *felt* it. She was healed and the power in him could only have been from God. But this God was not the horrible, punishing God that had been relentlessly presented to her. It was a God who allowed his people to touch him. He was a God who came down to the people's level. He was *her* God and he loved her as his daughter. He loved her every bit as much as Jairus loved his ailing daughter.

Later she heard that Jesus did an even greater miracle at Jairus' home that day. In fact, the little girl, who had been so seriously ill and was given up for dead, came round the next day with some delicious fresh bread and shared it with her. They had so much to talk about. There were still people in town that viewed the woman with suspicion and doubted her story. But she knew that her life had been changed that day. She also knew that should she ever feel such vulnerability again, this God of heaven who had come to earth was all the security she ever really needed. As his daughter, she was safe.

It is no wonder that this story is one of the most popular in the Bible. No one finds vulnerability comfortable, and we all instinctively want to shield ourselves and find good protection. So much can happen in life which makes us feel very unprotected – an alarming illness, a financial worry, the death of a good friend, hostile colleagues at work, to name just a few. But this story does introduce us to a God who stops and notices us when we feel our frailty and comes with a word that creates safety. The woman found healing as she let go of some old religious assumptions and judgements, and became open to a new vision of who God is. To be healed of her sickness was truly wonderful. But she might have told us that the greater wonder was to discover that a child of this earth could find true safety in this world of many threats.

Reflection

What makes you vulnerable? What makes you feel safe?

Prayer

Jesus, when I feel vulnerable in this world, let me touch the hem of your garment, that I may know your security.

CHANGE - SPACE FOR NEW VISION

Now the birth of Jesus the Messiah took place in this way. When his mother Mary had been engaged to Joseph, but before they lived together, she was found to be with child from the Holy Spirit. Her husband Joseph, being a righteous man and unwilling to expose her to public disgrace, planned to dismiss her quietly. But just when he had resolved to do this, an angel of the Lord appeared to him in a dream and said, 'Joseph, son of David, do not be afraid to take Mary as your wife, for the child conceived in her is from the Holy Spirit. She will bear a son, and you are to name him Jesus, for he will save his people from their sins.' All this took place to fulfil what had been spoken by the Lord through the prophet:
   'Look, the virgin shall conceive and bear a son,
      and they shall name him Emmanuel',
which means, 'God is with us.' When Joseph awoke from sleep, he did as the angel of the Lord commanded him; he took her as his wife, but had no marital relations with her until she had borne a son; and he named him Jesus.

MATTHEW 1:18–25 (see also MATTHEW 2)

Techniques on how to manage change are now big business, because it is widely recognised that, generally speaking, humans do not manage it well, and so we need help. To lead people through a process of change, you have to help them let go of something they find precious in order to embrace something new that they may know little about. People understandably find it difficult to abandon something they cherish if they are far from certain about what the future holds. It is okay if you have been part of choosing the change, but change that is foisted upon you can stir strong feelings of anger and resentment. The changes that are not of our making are often unwelcome. A redundancy means we have to change to a new job and perhaps a new town; children go to university and we have to face a home that is far too quiet without them; a church gets a new minister who changes much loved customs; someone we love becomes unexpectedly pregnant and our world changes dramatically. That was the change a first-century Nazarene carpenter had to face.

As far as we know, there was nothing to mark out Joseph from the other guys in town. Everyone was thrilled when he and Mary became betrothed – they seemed so right for each other. They were the perfect couple. Joseph was not wealthy, but he had a reasonable job with his woodcraft skills. Mary came from a good and respectable family. Life would change, of course, with marriage, but this was a change Joseph was looking forward to. But then came the change he was not expecting. Mary asked to meet with him privately and told him the devastating news that she was expecting a baby. In the culture of that day, it was nothing short of disastrous. A woman could be stoned to death for bearing a child out of wedlock. She said something to Joseph about it being God's, but the thought of God fathering a child in this world was wildly fanciful, not to say heretical. It was typical of Mary to try and make something spiritual out of a difficult situation. Joseph's skill was in crafting something useful out of an unpromising block of wood. Now, because he loved Mary, he had to craft a plan that would succeed in separating himself from Mary without her facing undue disgrace and distress. His world, which once looked so safe and good, has suddenly given way to a world of great uncertainty and full of threats.

Joseph finds it hard to sleep. He thinks about this problem day and night and can get no peace of mind. But, on this particular night, he at last falls into a sound sleep. His agitated body is finally still. The storm of worries of this terrible situation has temporarily been calmed. In the secret chambers of his mind, a dream is forming. It rises to that place just beneath the surface of consciousness. He finds himself in a place that feels sacred, for he senses a presence. He has felt it a few times in his life – the eerie yet beautiful sense of the closeness of something holy.

His body sleeps, but his soul has never been so alert as it is in these moments. In his dream world he turns, and there stands a creature more beautiful than he could dare to imagine. It is not a beauty to possess, but one to inspire him to better things. He is weeping as it speaks: 'Joseph, son of David.' He feels like his family history has been gathered up into this moment and offered before this holy creature. It speaks again and tells him that the life forming in the womb of his betrothed has been kindled by none other than the great Holy Spirit of God. His name is to be Jesus. The creature quotes a much-loved passage of scripture and says, 'God is with you.' Joseph has never felt God so close. It is in that moment of closeness that his mind slips into wakefulness with the sounds of heaven still ringing in his ears. He is changed.

Through this vision, Joseph is helped into a radically different view of the events that once seemed so disastrous. He lets go of his old views of God and how God works in this world. He lets go of his old view of Mary, and his old view of himself. As the sun rises over the Galilean hills, it is a different Joseph who walks calmly from his house to the home of Mary where, despite the shock of neighbours, he takes her as his wife and a remarkable journey of faith gets underway.

The autumn season of the soul is often marked by change, where we are letting go of something we once treasured to make space for something new. We need time to adjust to changes that come our way that are not of our choosing. Few of us will have night-time visitations of angels to help us, but the Joseph story tells us that there are heavenly resources to help with earthly problems. Another scripture tells us that we may have moments of entertaining angels without realising it.[11]

The messengers of God come in all kinds of ways as friends, texts, tweets, books, sunsets, smiles or, indeed, dreams. We need to be on the lookout for those signs of grace, sometimes detected by something just below the surface of our conscious self, an instinct that recognises the kindly work of God to direct us on to a new path. Once we know his company on that path, our tread will be that much more sure. Joseph did not necessarily find that new road an easy one, despite the help of the angels, but I suspect he never dreamed of going back to the old ways.

Reflection

How have you reacted to unwanted change that has come your way?

Prayer

Visit me, O Lord, in the deeper recesses of my soul that I may let go of the familiar path for the sake of the new.

HUMBLING – SPACE FOR GROWTH

But when Elisha the man of God heard that the king of Israel had torn his clothes, he sent a message to the king, 'Why have you torn your clothes? Let him come to me, that he may learn that there is a prophet in Israel.' So Naaman came with his horses and chariots, and halted at the entrance of Elisha's house. Elisha sent a messenger to him, saying, 'Go, wash in the Jordan seven times, and your flesh shall be restored and you shall be clean.' But Naaman became angry and went away, saying, 'I thought that for me he would surely come out, and stand and call on the name of the Lord his God, and would wave his hand over the spot, and cure the leprosy! Are not Abana and Pharpar, the rivers of Damascus, better than all the waters of Israel? Could I not wash in them, and be clean?' He turned and went away in a rage. But his servants approached and said to him, 'Father, if the prophet had commanded you to do something difficult, would you not have done it? How much more, when all he said to you was, "Wash, and be clean"?' So he went down and immersed himself seven times in the Jordan, according to the word of the man of God; his flesh was restored like the flesh of a young boy, and he was clean.

Then he returned to the man of God, he and all his company; he came and stood before him and said, 'Now I know that there is no God in all the earth except in Israel; please accept a present from your servant.'

2 KINGS 5:8–15 (see also all of 2 KINGS 5)

The most regular image of autumn is that of the dying leaf. Roads, lawns and pavements become strewn with an abundance of leaves discarded from their branches. In time these leaves are blown or swept away and, by the time spring bulbs break through the wintered earth, there is little sign of them. The discarded leaves are becoming humus, suitable for nourishing new life. The word 'humble' derives from the word 'humus' and there is a direct connection: the summer leaves, once proudly decorating the heights of the trees, are brought down to earth – they are humbled. In the seasons of the soul, any humbling can be painful, but as in the world of nature, such humbling can lead to remarkable new growth. Such was the case for a man called Naaman.

The story of Naaman takes us back to the ninth century BC. He is a commander in the army of the king of Aram, a neighbouring kingdom to Israel. Despite his seniority, he is not immune to the diseases that afflict all humans, and at some point in his life, he becomes infected with the dreaded and unsightly disease of leprosy. However, Naaman's wife had acquired a servant girl from Israel, and this girl spoke of a prophet back in her homeland called Elisha, who has been known to cure people of this disease. Naaman's ears understandably prick up at this news, and he follows important protocols by asking his king to prepare a letter of introduction for him to take to the king of Israel. The Aramean monarch obliges and off goes Naaman, grasping his official letter and a handy amount of gold, silver and expensive clothes with which to butter up the king of Israel.

It wasn't a bad plan, but it nearly hits disaster when the king of Israel opens the letter, which is not very clearly written, for it implies that *he* should cure Naaman of his leprosy. Surely the king of Aram knows that regal powers do not extend to curing diseases. So he begins to suspect that this is all a ploy to get another war going. However, news reaches the ears of Elisha just in time, who saves the day by offering his services.

Naaman is relieved the misunderstanding is resolved, and heads off to Elisha's house. However, when he gets there he hits a major blow to his pride. As he waits by the front door of Elisha's house, a messenger comes out with a directive that if Naaman wants to be cured, he must go and wash in the Jordan seven times. This is getting close to the last straw for Naaman. Not only is he humiliated by having this unsightly disease in the first place, but he also has to go and get help from a foreign country. Now, he finds a prophet who can help but hasn't got the common decency to come to his front door and speak to him personally. Naaman is exasperated. Why should he plunge himself in this nasty foreign river when he could bathe in the bright streams of his homeland? It is the humble servants who eventually manage to persuade him to swallow his pride and at least give the recommended remedy a try.

So Naaman rides off to the nearby river and dismounts his horse near a still part of the water. One of his servants unbuckles his sandals, for Naaman's numb and misshapen hands are past accomplishing such delicate tasks. He steps towards the cool water and wades in. He stops when the water reaches his waist. From the calm flat surface of the dark water, a face looks back at him, and he sees what he has tried to avoid: the ugly evidence of this fearful disease. For a few moments he wonders if the leprosy is affecting his brain. Does he honestly think that by stepping into this water his face, arms and hands will be made whole again? He imagines the scene of people at home beside themselves with mirth at the story of the great commander who thought his leprosy would be cured by having a dip in a foreign river. But so much pride has been lost now. He might as well go through with it. He strikes the water and the trembling image distorts and fragments.

He feels the current tugging at him. It feels as if there is a new, unknown current shifting his mind and soul. He takes a deep breath and down he goes into the watery world of muted sounds. He stays fully submerged for as long as he can manage, and then rises, gasping and hoping. He looks at his hands but there is no change.

Down he goes again – and again, and again. His servants are waiting in silence on the riverbank with looks of such beckoning hope. For the seventh and final time, Naaman plunges under the water. He opens his eyes under the water and looks at his outstretched hands. He turns them round to study their backs. Can it be? They look different! They are not the gnarled, lumpy hands that scarcely had the strength to grip a cup, let alone a commander's sword. Is the lack of oxygen damaging his mind?

He rises from the water and draws his dripping hands up to his face. He can scarcely dare believe what he sees – not only is there no sign of the dreaded leprosy, but his hands look like they belong to a youngster! He hesitantly touches his face and there is feeling in his cheeks again, and none of the unsightly lumps. He moves to the stiller part of the water's edge and looks down at the swaying reflection of young skin. His feet feel strong as he strides out of the river towards his delighted servants. He looks back, fastening this river scene into his mind. For the rest of his life he will remember this day, as the day when he drowned his considerable pride and met with a God whose healing swirled around him and delivered him from this fearful illness. A world of new possibilities has opened to him.

Naaman took considerable risks in choosing humility over pride. He might have ended up becoming the laughing stock of two countries. But had he stuck to his pride, he would never have found his healing. Perhaps it was desperation that caused him to give up his pride and head down to that river. But there was perhaps another driver. Over 800 years later, Jesus began his ministry by going into the local synagogue of his home town of Nazareth and shocked the people by preaching a somewhat radical sermon which resulted in his nearly been thrown off a cliff. One of the things that scandalised that prim and proper synagogue was Jesus' choice of an example of radiant faith. Neatly bypassing all those people with proper credentials such as Abraham and Moses, he chose two Gentiles, one of whom was none other than our Commander Naaman. Because of Naaman's extraordinary faith, rooted simply in the hunch of a servant girl and the word of a discourteous prophet, he discovered a whole new vitality in his life. Being humbled in this world is never comfortable, but with a little faith, it can often make space for new growth to flourish in our lives.

Reflection

Why is it often difficult to take the humble way? What is it that we lose? But what might we gain?

Prayer

Lord, when I am humbled in life help me to find the waters of faith that I might find my freedom.

DISTURBANCE – SPACE FOR A NEW CALLING

The words of Nehemiah son of Hacaliah. In the month of Chislev, in the twentieth year, while I was in Susa the capital, one of my brothers, Hanani, came with certain men from Judah; and I asked them about the Jews that survived, those who had escaped the captivity, and about Jerusalem. They replied, 'The survivors there in the province who escaped captivity are in great trouble and shame; the wall of Jerusalem is broken down, and its gates have been destroyed by fire.'

When I heard these words I sat down and wept, and mourned for days, fasting and praying before the God of heaven. I said, 'O Lord God of heaven, the great and awesome God who keeps covenant and steadfast love with those who love him and keep his commandments; let your ear be attentive and your eyes open to hear the prayer of your servant that I now pray before you day and night for your servants the people of Israel, confessing the sins of the people of Israel, which we have sinned against you. Both I and my family have sinned… O Lord, let your ear be attentive to the prayer of your servant, and to the prayer of your servants who delight in revering your name. Give success to your servant today, and grant him mercy in the sight of this man!'

NEHEMIAH 1:1–6, 11

It is hard to get through a day without being disturbed by something. Among the usual disturbances of family, work and finances, there are the disturbances of world events that come as reports through our news channels. While we may do our best to brush these to one side, there are occasions where the thing that disturbs us has no intention of being so easily dismissed. It stubbornly persists in catching our attention and conversing with us. Such a disturbance is one that carries a calling, and usually a calling that brings about a sense of autumnal vulnerability, where we feel exposed and ill equipped.

Nehemiah knew all about this. We are back in the fifth century BC in the days of the Persian Empire. Over 100 years before, Nehemiah's ancestors had been driven out of Jerusalem by foreign armies, and the survivors were captured and exiled. As time went by and new generations came on the scene, the feelings for the old country grew weaker. However, tides of homesickness still visited those Hebrew people who kept hold of their scriptures, their God and their traditions. They nursed their wound but no one knew what to do about their once glorious city that was now abandoned and in ruins.

Nehemiah held a senior position in the court of the Persian King Artaxerxes I. The book of the Bible that bears his name gets to the point straight away. We are in the month of Chislev, which is in the late autumn. It was sometimes called 'the month of dreams', and that certainly became the case for Nehemiah. He is a devout man and I imagine him dutifully going about his business in the court of the king. But there are already signs of disturbance in his heart, even though he can't quite put his finger on what it is.

Then one day, in the palace at Susa, he is sitting at his desk by the window, with the low sun highlighting his neatly cut, greying beard, when there is a knock at the door. He rises and opens it, and there is the familiar sight of his brother, Hanani, who has come with a group of men who are strangers to Nehemiah. He welcomes them into the rather grand room that serves as his office. He calls for some wine and invites his visitors to sit on the elaborate stone bench that is backed by a colourful tapestry. Hanani tells his brother that these men are from his homeland. That first reference to home causes Nehemiah to raise an eyebrow as he sits back down at his sunlit wooden desk. He leans forwards, clasping his hands and fixing his eyes on these new guests. How is the ancient city of Jerusalem?

The wine arrives and fine goblets are passed around the room as Hanani's friends tell of the once great city of the people of Israel. They spare no details, each one chipping in one horrific detail after another, painting a dismal scene of a city bereft of its former glory and stagnating as a ruin, making a mockery of the faith that once caused it to be so great. The sun-glinted goblet of wine stands untouched on Nehemiah's desk. He feels his present world is fading from him as his soul ventures into this other world so painfully detailed by these new friends. The story is awakening an unfamiliar emotion. He feels it first as a fluttering in his chest. He is one of the senior people in this palace, always careful to control his emotions, but something powerful is threatening to shatter this professional resistance. It shows first in his face, which contorts into a grimace. A grief, which feels much more than his own personal grief, is too powerful for even his resistance. Large tears break and fall to the desk while his hand instinctively rises to his mouth. He presses his knuckles to his teeth, as if such an action could hold back the force of such emotion.

He grasps the goblet, and drops of spilt wine mix with tears on the ancient desk. He gulps at the wine, hoping it will in some way provide healing to his wounded soul, but he knows that nothing will shift this aching grief for the city of God. Hanani can see that his brother needs solitude, so he and his friends make their way out, bowing as they go.

Nehemiah wipes his face on the sleeve of his robe and then paces up and down his room. His soul is in chaos, and he becomes acutely aware of the deep wound in his homeless people. Humbly, he does not sidestep his own part in this. As far as he can see, he is part of this mess, but in acknowledging this he realises that he can also be part of the healing. He gives the days that follow to fasting and prayer, and in time the nightmare becomes a dream: from the deep inner disturbance comes a sense of call. He must go and inspect the city himself. And this is the beginning of a great change of direction for Nehemiah. The king consents to this new adventure, and Nehemiah is soon on his way to Jerusalem, embarking on a grand plan of reconstruction that will restore his beloved city.

Every day we are bombarded with stories of tragedy, whether in our own neighbourhoods, or from far-off, unfamiliar lands. Usually we find ways of emotionally managing these, but occasionally we hear a story that crawls under our skin and, like with Nehemiah, it becomes a productive disturbance. A passion begins to burn and a vision unfurls that might seem ridiculous, yet will not be ridiculed. We release our protective leaves and become vulnerably open. We spend time on our knees because we know we are not up to what is required. It is here that we become aware of a call of God, beckoning us to work for rebuilding and healing in a part of his wounded world. A friend of mine called Sundar is from India and lives in Derbyshire. He thought he was always going to be an economist until one day he flicked on his TV and caught a news report from his home state about an orphan girl. Like Nehemiah, Sundar's soul was besieged by sorrow and distress, but after his own time of mourning and prayer it became clear this was the disturbance of a call of God. He and his wife gave up their safe and prosperous world. They tracked down that little girl, and set about building an orphanage for her and others in her plight. It is now a flourishing home for many rescued children.[12]

We may not like autumns of disturbance, but they may well be times when we are shaken out of our comfortable, leafy worlds, and space is created in which we hear a new calling. This can be one of the great gifts of autumn.

Reflection

What is disturbing you? Is there a message in the disturbance you need to hear?

Prayer

Lord, give me ears to hear the message in the disturbance.

WINTER

The season of
discovery

INTRODUCTION

If you ask someone in modern-day Britain what comes to mind when you mention the season of winter, most will probably refer to things like dark nights, dark mornings and even whole days of dark, when the clouds are so dense you wonder if the sun has actually made it above the horizon at all. In addition, there will probably be comments about freezing temperatures, travel disruptions and fuel bills. Some may refer to the leafless trees and the animals escaping underground to their hidden world of hibernation. But there will be not only reports of bad news: people will also mention beautiful snowflakes, thrilling toboggan rides, striking landscapes and of course the bright festival of Christmas. As with all seasons, winter is a mixed blessing, but of all the seasons it is probably the one that is least favoured. Our language betrays our instinctive feelings about the seasons: we talk about the 'height of summer' and the 'dead of winter'. For those of us who love the warmth and light of summer days, we have to learn to appreciate the different kind of light that winter has to offer.

In early Celtic times, winter (*Samhain*) was seen to begin on 1 November with the darkest of the days falling in the middle of the season before the slow recovery of the light in January. For those early Celts, this was a dangerous season. In part, this was due to the belief that, with the dark overtaking the light, it was the time when the powers of darkness grew more influential. The spirits of the underworld took advantage of the absence of light. When the Christians started to impact these early cultures in Europe, they noticed the dread of this season, and so they planted All Saints Day right at the start of it to move the people from fearing the spirits of darkness to celebrating the saints of light. They also chose the darkest time of the year to be the season to celebrate God entering this world as the babe of Bethlehem, and to proclaim loud and clear the gospel message that 'the light shines in the darkness, and the darkness did not overcome it'.[13]

Even when they were emboldened by the gospel of light, those early Celtic peoples couldn't shield themselves completely from the ravages of winter, from which generally nowadays we are well defended. If you were sick, elderly or physically vulnerable in any way, winter was a dangerous time for you. Many lives came to an end in the dead of winter.

The soul also knows its wintry seasons and can suffer from its own form of a seasonally affected disorder. That lack of light can be caused by all kinds of life experiences, and most suffering of this world will be experienced as a wintery season in our lives. In Christian spirituality, the term 'the dark night of the soul' is well known and was coined by the 16th-century Spanish mystic, John of the Cross.[14] In his personal experience of suffering, he unearthed what the prophet Isaiah called, 'the treasures of the darkness'.[15] You would think that the cold, gloomy night has little to offer, yet these mystics like John reported that even in the darkest places there could be exceptional discoveries, not least the bright, warm love of God. John's words in one of his poems capture this:

O night, that guided me!
O night, sweeter than sunrise!
O night, that joined lover with Beloved!
Lover transformed in Beloved![16]

It is this paradox that makes the winter season of the soul one that is full of possibility. The peoples of the Bible were no strangers to wintry experiences of suffering. But, as we shall see, there were those who showed openness, courage and determination that enabled them to discern the treasures of God in the most unpromising circumstances. Such treasure makes the winter season one of adventure and discovery.

DEATH – THE DISCOVERY OF PREVAILING LOVE

In the days when the judges ruled, there was a famine in the land, and a certain man of Bethlehem in Judah went to live in the country of Moab, he and his wife and two sons. The name of the man was Elimelech and the name of his wife Naomi, and the names of his two sons were Mahlon and Chilion; they were Ephrathites from Bethlehem in Judah. They went into the country of Moab and remained there. But Elimelech, the husband of Naomi, died, and she was left with her two sons. These took Moabite wives; the name of one was Orpah and the name of the other Ruth. When they had lived there for about ten years, both Mahlon and Chilion also died, so that the woman was left without her two sons or her husband.

RUTH 1:1–5 (see also all of RUTH)

It is the thing we dread: the quivering voice on the phone from an Accident and Emergency Department; the fateful look of the specialist as she delivers the results; the black-coated men grimly drawing the coffin from the hearse; the half-worn toothbrush that no one can bear to clear away; the tear-washed photo clutched to the breast; the dull, dull ache of grief; the fear-filled world of unimaginable loss; the dreadful visitation of death.

Most humans encounter the bitter reality of death in this world early on in their lives. If you are fortunate, you might make it into your middle years before you encounter one of the terrible severe griefs of losing one of your closest loves. But sooner or later it comes – a death of someone close to you – and nothing has prepared you for managing the acute sense of loss that now fills every part of your life.

And if it is not you that is going through this dark night of grief, then it is probable that during most of your days on this earth, you are not too far from someone you know who is stumbling through the dark valley of mourning.

So what do we do with all the death that keeps making its ugly presence felt in our world? And where does God fit into it? How come he allows so many untimely and unfair deaths? These are questions that have been explored by humans from the earliest of times, and they are questions that are very evident in the story of Ruth.

The book of Ruth is one that begins with a natural disaster and soon progresses to an acute experience of family grief. A couple called Elimelech and Naomi take the reasonable decision to flee their famine-struck homeland and they make their way east to Moab with their two sons. This is a journey that tells us just how desperate they were, for there existed deep suspicion between the nations of Judah and Moab. Their history was littered with appalling massacres perpetrated between one nation and the other. Nonetheless, Elimelech and his family manage to settle in the one-time hostile land. But their peace is soon shattered when Elimelech dies.

Naomi is now a migrant widow and very vulnerable. But she does have her boys. It is going to take years for their homeland to recover from the famine, so they settle down in Moab, and soon the boys marry local women, despite the fact that if folks at home knew about these mixed marriages, they would have been hounded out of town. For the next ten years, all is relatively well, until a further tragedy afflicts the family: the two men die. Naomi is the last member of the original family left. It is not surprising that she develops a longing for the safety of her homeland, so when the famine is over, she decides to return to Judah.

Off she sets with her two Moabite daughters-in-law. At some point on that journey, she becomes seriously worried about how life will be for these two women who will find themselves foreigners in Israel.

Thus we get a poignant roadside conversation in the first chapter of Ruth that reveals the depth of love and care that these three women have for one another. Their shared suffering has bound them together. Orpah eventually chooses to remain in Moab, but Ruth has decided that her devotion to her mother-in-law is so deep that she wants to stick with her, come what may. So, with much weeping Naomi and Ruth bid farewell to Orpah, and the two grieving women make their way to Bethlehem.

We see these two widows making their way into Naomi's hometown. As they arrive at the edge of town, Naomi is immediately recognised, and word quickly goes round that an old and frail Naomi has lost her husband and sons and has returned with a young Moabite woman. The two women slowly walk into the centre of town and Ruth grasps Naomi's arm even more tightly as she sees the suspicion on the faces of the onlookers.

A woman who has been doing some washing at a nearby well is one of Naomi's old friends. She puts down her laundry and comes over with a broad smile on her face. She calls out 'Naomi!' and is about to embrace her, when Naomi puts up her hand in defiance of the hug, and says, 'Don't call me Naomi any more.' In the original language, her name means 'pleasant', with the sense that she is one who pleases God and others. But with her life now defined by grief and bad fortune, Naomi can no longer own this name.

The old friend takes Naomi and Ruth over to the well, and they sit beside it in the afternoon light. A few others gather around, curious to hear more of this tragic story. The friend passes a water-filled gourd for the women, who gladly refresh themselves. 'Call me "Bitter",' says Naomi, 'for the Almighty has afflicted me. I was once so full, and my life is now so empty.' She turns her head sharply away, ashamed of the tears that have flowed so unremittingly in these dark days. Ruth brushes the hair from her mother-in-law's eyes and says some reassuring words. The friend notices however that the Moabite, the foreigner and one-time enemy, has great love in her heart for her mother-in-law. As Ruth gratefully passes back the gourd, the friend sees a quality in her dignified face. Only later does she realise that it is the quality of hope – a resolute hope born from a heart of devoted love.

If you read on in this story, you will discover that life gets a lot better for Ruth and Naomi. A relative of Elimelech by the name of Boaz comes on to the scene and it is not long before he falls for the Moabite widow and, despite the disapproving looks of those who believed that all decent people would not go anywhere near a foreigner, he takes her for his wife. It's not long before Ruth gives birth to a boy whom they call Obed. In a touching end to the book of Ruth, we see the neighbours gathering round not Ruth, but Naomi, who cradles her grandson in her arms. They remind her that she may have suffered a severe tragedy in her life, but through it all she has found Ruth who, they claim, is better than seven sons.[17] That's quite a thing to say about someone who is supposed to be your sworn enemy. But this is just what raw human grief does to a community. It profoundly disturbs all who are in its wake. On the one hand, it can reinforce old prejudices and false views. Naomi concluded from her tragedy that God and the people viewed her as 'bitter'. But grief affects Ruth differently – though her heart was so desperately hurt by the loss of her husband, she kept the stream of love open to Naomi, and to the people of Bethlehem despite their mistrust of her because of her ethnic roots.

There is no easy way to travel on the road of grief. But Ruth invites us to follow the way of the open heart. There was a generosity in her heart that allowed the seeds of hope to grow. She did not permit her grief to make her bitter, and she found in her soul a way to love, and that love had its healing effect not just on her but on Naomi and indeed on the people of Bethlehem as well.

When Matthew embarked on the writing of his Gospel, he decided to begin it by recording for us a lengthy ancestry of Jesus. This is made up of almost entirely male names. However, standing proud in that crowd of males is Ruth the mother of Obed. Perhaps he felt we should know that Jesus had something of the stuff of Ruth in him – that capacity to love, come what may.[18] Death will always be an enemy to humans. But Ruth shows us that it need not have the last word.

Reflection

How do we love in times of grief?

Prayer

There is a God whose light shines in every darkness
There is a God who hears every lament
There is a God who transforms even the deepest grief
Therefore you have hope:
You shall sing again, but with a different tune
You shall dance again, but with a different step
You shall laugh again, but with a different breath
Not yet, but one day,
For there is a God who heals your wound with the gentlest hand.[19]

GUILT – THE DISCOVERY OF WISDOM

Have mercy on me, O God,
    according to your steadfast love;
according to your abundant mercy
    blot out my transgressions.
Wash me thoroughly from my iniquity,
    and cleanse me from my sin.

For I know my transgressions,
    and my sin is ever before me.
Against you, you alone, have I sinned,
    and done what is evil in your sight,
so that you are justified in your sentence
    and blameless when you pass judgement.

PSALM 51:1–4 (see also all of PSALM 51; 2 SAMUEL 11:1–25)

From a very early age, we experience guilt. We discover it around the time we find that the world is full of rules – things we are supposed to do and things we are most definitely not supposed to do. We face the choice of compliance or rebellion. We weigh up the risks of breaking the rules. We develop devices for avoiding the expected disapproval or punishment that comes with breaking the rules. At first we are not very good at it, as we haven't learned to conceal signs of our crimes such as telltale chocolate marks on our cheeks. It takes a little while to learn how to deceive parents and carers. But even if we do manage to deceive and avoid the punishments and disapprovals, there can remain an uncomfortable feeling within that is called 'guilt'. Laws and rules vary from culture to culture and perceptions of what is wrong can change. But whatever the outer norms of behaviour, there is somewhere in the human heart an instinctive recognition when we have done or said something that is not right, good or true. When that happens, it leaves a bitter taste that can last a long time.

Some people are terribly burdened by their guilt, even carrying it over many years, finding it hard to resolve. Others work hard to ignore this instinct, yet find there are those moments in life when something or someone manages to lift the lid of that instinct and they are faced with the stark facts of their own wrongdoing. Such an uncomfortable discovery happened in the life of the great King David, who is hailed as one of the greatest and most saintly of our Bible characters, yet was not without his faults.

It all began with an evening walk and a fateful glance in the direction of a young woman taking a bath. David has been king in Jerusalem for about ten years, and all is going very well in his kingdom. He is becoming powerful, and is getting used to having his own way. As he secretly views this bathing beauty, he sees no reason why he shouldn't have her in his bed. He is the king, after all. She may be married but, so he thinks, she would probably far rather sleep with a great king. Thus she is summoned to his bedroom and he has his way with her.

Inconveniently, she becomes pregnant after this liaison, so this presents a tricky problem. However, David comes up with a cunning plan that should protect him from being found out: firstly, get her husband Uriah to sleep with her as soon as possible, so people will think the baby is his. Then, because he would like to keep Bathsheba, he finds a way of getting rid of Uriah without a trace of suspicion. There's a battle coming up and, as Uriah is a soldier, David gets him put in the front line to ensure he is killed. The plan works a treat as Uriah is handily killed in battle. David feigns distress at the loss of Uriah, and as an act of great kindness takes the grieving wife into his palace to care for her. The plan works brilliantly. No one suspects a thing. No one that is, except a tiresome prophet called Nathan.

David wakes up on a beautiful morning and his lovely Bathsheba is in the palace nursery feeding their newborn son. He feels on top of the world, apart from a rather nagging discomfort in his spirit that he prefers to ignore. At breakfast he is enjoying some fresh peaches and fine grapes, when a servant ushers in his good friend, Nathan the prophet. David offers him a peach, which the prophet declines. He sits near David, who reaches for his cup. Nathan begins, 'I have a story to tell you, your highness.' David loves stories and sits back in his chair and noisily sucks the juice from a peach.

The prophet tells the story of a certain town in which lived a rich man and a poor man. The rich man had a large number of sheep and cattle, but the poor man could only afford one ewe lamb. This poor man loved this ewe lamb greatly, as did his children. She became one of the family and would even sleep alongside them. Then one day, the rich man received a visitor. The visitor needed feeding, but instead of using one of his own lambs for the meal, the rich man took, of all things, the poor man's beloved ewe.

At this point in the story, David is enraged. He thumps the table with his fist and says, 'That rich man deserves to die for such a thing!' In fact, he goes on at some length detailing the punishments that should be meted out on this disreputable character. When he has finished, Nathan pauses for a few moments. He then looks hard at David, lifts his finger and pointing at him says, 'You are the man.' The words thunder into David's heart. He immediately knows the game is up. Nathan is after all a prophet – perhaps he should have guessed. Nathan details the full list of David's crimes, which includes breaking the sixth, seventh, ninth and tenth commandments[20] – a pretty impressive collection of sins. As David is reeling from the shock of being found out, Nathan leans forward and then says, 'And the sentence, your highness, will be severe. I am sorry, but there has to be something.' The old prophet grasps the shaking hand of the king for, though he is the prophet delivering a harsh message, he is also a dear friend.

David's face reddens and contorts in anguish and horror. He has a choice – to defend himself and make excuses, or accept that he is responsible. His watery eyes look up to Nathan. In a quivering voice he says, 'I have sinned against the Lord.' The prophet kneels next to the sobbing king, their wet faces pressed together in desperation.

We understand that Psalm 51 was composed by David and is his beautifully written, heartfelt expression of guilt. The whole episode was undoubtedly a severe winter for the soul of David. But in the darkness, he did find some treasures. He discovered that his God loved him come what may, for his opening words are an appeal for mercy 'according to *your steadfast love*' (v. 1). He also discovered that though guilt can wound the soul, it can also cause us to examine our inner life. 'You desire truth in the *inward being*,' prays David, so 'teach me wisdom in my *secret heart*' (v. 6). This is the place where true conscience resides. David discovered the therapeutic forgiveness of God, and he became a wiser and more understanding king.

By any reckoning, Psalm 51 is a remarkable piece of writing. It's hard to imagine a modern-day monarch or leader publishing something like this. They would feel far too exposed – imagine what the press would make of it! But David was so committed to nurturing his inner life that he was prepared to share his stories of faults and failures to help us all into greater degrees of honesty. When we bring our guilt to the steadfast love of God, there is always hope that we will grow in wisdom.

Reflection

What do you do with your guilt?

Prayer

Create in me a clean heart, O God and put a new and right spirit within me.

DESPAIR - THE DISCOVERY OF HOPE

By the rivers of Babylon –
   there we sat down and there we wept
   when we remembered Zion.
On the willows there
   we hung up our harps.
For there our captors
   asked us for songs,
and our tormentors asked for mirth, saying,
   'Sing us one of the songs of Zion!'

How could we sing the Lord's song
   in a foreign land?

PSALM 137:1–4 (see also all of PSALM 137; ISAIAH 40)

We see it too often on screen, magazine and newspaper: a city of canvas stretches off to the distance; men who once laughed and joked with workmates, now stand arms-folded and solemn-faced gazing at the high fence; a child dressed in foreign clothes lugs a plastic tub of water across the dusty ground; a woman sits on her haunches stirring a thin soup. The issue of refugees is centuries old – families uprooted from their once stable homes are forced to exist in transience and poverty until that blessed day when they can find a land of safety and belonging. Most find themselves in this plight because of the brutality of their fellow humans. It has to be one of the most severe forms of human winters.

The inhabitants of sixth-century BC Jerusalem knew this winter story only too well. The powerful ruler Nebuchadnezzar had ransacked their city and dragged them off through the desert to the foreign city of Babylon. It was there that one of their poets wrote a most beautiful psalm. Just the first line catches the utter poignancy and desolation of their situation: 'By the rivers of Babylon, there we sat down and there we wept.' They are exhausted with weeping. They torture themselves with the memories of better days. Their captors also taunt them to add insult to terrible injury. The songs that used to give them such courage and cheer have now dried up and have got stuck in their throats. They are a people for whom hope has died. All that stirs them now are ugly thoughts of vengeance (see the appalling v. 9). It is a desperate situation. That word 'desperate' means literally 'without hope'.

One day a prophet comes into that world, the author of the 40th chapter of the book of Isaiah. No one really knows for sure who wrote these middle chapters of the book of Isaiah, but most reckon that chapter 40 marks the beginning of a section of writing that was primarily addressed to the exiles in Babylon. This writer was building on the message so clearly articulated by the prophet Isaiah in the first part of the book. I have often imagined this prophet dwelling in that camp of exiled Israelites by the waters of Babylon.

I see him as an older man, for he has needed a good quantity of years behind him to allow for the fermenting of wisdom. He has always been a bit aloof in that camp. He has had a different look in his eye to the others. He's a watcher, an observer. He has been seen standing for hours just looking out beyond the high wooden fence of the camp. He stands like a sentry in his long robe, and his arms hang at his side. There is serenity in him, yet also profound energy revealed in the way his fingers frequently stir and twitch. He seems to be on the lookout for something. So when he eventually does turn round from his watch and opens his mouth in speech, the words that come from his lips sound like they come from another world, and in many respects they do.

His opening words are the words each and every person in that camp is desperate to hear: 'Comfort' (Isaiah 40:1). There is nothing of comfort in this camp, and no words have yet brought comfort. But this prophet has found something, and that something does have a note of consolation about it. Off he goes around that camp, speaking to those who want to hear. His words are astonishing. His eyes glitter like the river beside the camp, only the glint in his eye is not from the sun but from another kind of light. Down those rows of tents he goes, and his voice rises over the murmured conversations: 'Every valley shall be lifted up... the uneven ground shall become level' (Isaiah 40:4). Even in this dark desert of a place, 'the glory of the Lord shall be revealed' (Isaiah 40:5).

He delivers what he has been hearing in his soul – the word of God erupts from him. The men turn from staring at the high fence as if they are emerging from a stupor; the child puts down that heavy tub of water and a long-lost whimsical smile returns; the woman moves the pan from the fire and gets to her feet while her eyes fill with different tears. The prophet's words stay ringing not just in their ears but in their hearts: 'those who wait for the Lord shall... mount up with wings like eagles' (Isaiah 40:31).

Not all of them, but many of them were transformed by that message. The prophet delivered to them a message of extraordinary hope birthed from his deep, painful listening. It began with a declaration of the tender love of God. It helped them to shift their view of God, from that of a deity who was out to get them to a tender shepherd feeding his flock (see v. 11). They began to grasp the fact that even this apparently desperate situation was not without hope. Some of those people did eventually make their way back to Jerusalem. Some stayed in Babylon and learned to flourish there. And over 400 years later a wild prophet in the Judean desert blazoned those words again to a people terribly oppressed by political and religious rulers. He was called John the Baptist, and he introduced to the world a radical rabbi who turned out to be a saviour. As John poured water on the head of this rabbi Jesus in the river Jordan, a voice from heaven proclaimed him as his much-beloved son. This son was in exile on earth, away from the perfect home of paradise. And yet his life in exile transformed this world, and lives of despair have found hope.

When we hit times of hopelessness, Isaiah 40 is a great tonic. It tells us there is another way of looking at things. When in August 1941 the brilliant scientist and faithful priest Father Maximilian Kolbe was left to die in an underground bunker in Auschwitz with ten other men, what astonished the guards more than anything was the sound of singing coming from that dark subterranean cell. Maximilian saw things differently. He had to let go of old hopes and, by releasing them, he made space for something quite revolutionary. He plucked his lyre from the tree, so to speak, and sang the Lord's song in that bleakest of foreign lands. Those lives in that cruel cell ended far too soon. And yet in those days they perhaps learned to live in such a way that makes most of our lives look pale by comparison.

All kinds of despairs and disappointments can come our way in life and can lead us into a wintry gloom. But Isaiah, Maximilian and countless others through history and indeed around us today demonstrate that such experiences can lead us to catch sight of a different vision. Hope comes from the willingness to see things differently. The eagle's eye is among the strongest in the animal kingdom. Those who wait upon the Lord, to use the language of Isaiah 40, may well find they are not only given the wings of the eagle, but its eyes as well. It is the seeing from those eyes that brings genuine hope.

Reflection

Find Isaiah 40 and read it through slowly. Breathe it into your heart. Read it not so much to understand it but to *feel* it.

Prayer

When my spirit is low, Lord, grant my soul the eyes and the wings of the eagle.

FAILURE – THE DISCOVERY OF BEING

[Jesus] came to a Samaritan city called Sychar, near the plot of ground that Jacob had given to his son Joseph. Jacob's well was there, and Jesus, tired out by his journey, was sitting by the well. It was about noon.

A Samaritan woman came to draw water, and Jesus said to her, 'Give me a drink'. (His disciples had gone to the city to buy food.) The Samaritan woman said to him, 'How is it that you, a Jew, ask a drink of me, a woman of Samaria?' (Jews do not share things in common with Samaritans.) Jesus answered her, 'If you knew the gift of God, and who it is that is saying to you, "Give me a drink", you would have asked him, and he would have given you living water...' Jesus said to her, 'Go, call your husband, and come back.' The woman answered him, 'I have no husband.' Jesus said to her, 'You are right in saying, "I have no husband"; for you have had five husbands, and the one you have now is not your husband. What you have said is true!' The woman said to him, 'Sir, I see that you are a prophet.

JOHN 4:5–10, 16–19 (see also JOHN 4:1–42)

What do Frank Sinatra, Kate Winslett, Muhammed Ali, Jennifer Lopez, Halle Berry and Tom Cruise all have in common? Answer: they have all been married three times or more. And they are not alone in this experience. While we may feel some sorrow in hearing of these marital breakdowns, there is seldom a sense of shame about it in our modern western culture. But in other cultures it would be very different, and go back 2,000 years into the first-century Middle East and such breakdowns would be viewed with great suspicion and disapproval.

The woman who features in this story from John's Gospel would certainly give many celebrities a run for their money in this regard: she's been through five husbands and she now seems to have given up on the idea of marriage and has settled for cohabitation. She is the central figure of a story that comes early on in John's Gospel. We know nothing about the reasons for all these marriage breakdowns, and to what extent she was responsible or a victim. In the culture of the day, which always favoured male rights over female, the general populace would certainly have taken a very dim view of her. It is reasonable to suppose that in terms of human relationships she must have felt a dismal failure. Yet her conversation with Jesus reveals her as someone who didn't allow that sense of failure to rob her of her longings, and we meet her as someone who is confident and feisty.

Jesus often rode roughshod over the social and religious conventions of the day especially when they caused the more vulnerable to suffer. One strongly held convention was that Jewish men (particularly rabbis) should not go anywhere near a Samaritan woman (particularly those who have multiple failed marriages behind them). But this is just the kind of situation that interested Jesus. And this is why he got into a conversation with the Samaritan woman from Sychar.

The woman has to choose her time carefully to go up to the well. Due to her personal circumstances, people don't want to associate with her. So she has to go in the heat of the day, while others go when it is cooler. Much to her annoyance, she sees a man sitting there. She is not supposed to go near a man in public, but she has broken so many conventions by now, one more offence won't make much difference. She labours along the hot rocky path to the sound of singing cicadas. She skilfully carries her large water pot. She can tell that the man sitting on the side of the well is not one of her people – he is one of the Jews. Even more reason for him to despise her, so she supposes.

He watches her as she makes her way to the well. She expects him to move when he sees her coming, for surely he won't want to be tainted by this foreign woman. But to her surprise, he remains. As she arrives, she puts down her water pot and aims to haul up the bucket from the well for some welcome fresh water. 'Could you give me a drink?' asks the stranger. The woman is astounded – a man speaking to a woman in public? But if he is a rule-breaker and wants a conversation, well, why not make the most of it?

She stands by the seated Jewish man and shades her eyes with one hand and places the other on her hip. They start a conversation about water, and her heart brightens. She discovers this man is a rabbi – a rabbi who is happy to talk to a woman about matters of God. Her eager, enquiring mind has longed for this. He points down the well and tells her of a different kind of well that is full to the brim with heavenly water. She knows this is the water for which she has thirsted for so long. 'Give me this water, please!' she cries in delight.

But then the man darkens the conversation with a reference to the story for which she is so derided: her relationships with men. It seems he is a seer and he knows about the five marriages, and he knows about the man with whom she lives. And yet, she will not allow this to ruin such a life-giving conversation. She swiftly diverts the discussion to a controversial subject to do with the technically correct location for a true worship of God. As he speaks about worship, she draws closer to take a closer look at this Jewish leader. He does not turn his head away from her gaze. It is as if she recognises him – it feels as if he is someone for whom she has been searching for many years. Indeed, she feels, he is someone for whom all people have been searching.

'The… the Messiah is coming,' she says in a voice broken by emotion. He continues his kindly gaze and says, 'I am he – the one who is speaking to you now. You need look no further.' She needs no convincing. She would love to talk further, but is annoyed by the arrival of a group of men who seem to know this rabbi. They look disapproving. She wants no one to spoil this sacred moment, so she abruptly leaves, forgetting her water pot. Jesus watches her making her way excitedly along the path to her hometown and he chuckles in contentment.

John, the storyteller, writes that she returned home after this conversation and, despite her reputation, many were fascinated to hear her story. Her testimony had an extraordinary impact on the people and indeed on millions since. When Jesus met with her by that well, he was perhaps the first man to take her questions and insights seriously, and was not prejudiced by her gender or her life story. Her failed relationships and the social stigma attached to them could have left her in a permanent winter of bitterness and regret. But she never let go of her longing for life, and so when she met someone who led her to a well of living water, she gladly drew from it. She gained a new sense of identity – a new sense of being and of purpose.

If we had bumped into this Samaritan woman on her way back from the well that afternoon, we might have asked her just what it was about her conversation with the foreign rabbi that caused such a change in her heart. My guess is that her answer would run something along these lines: 'Others may have written me off as a failure and of having no opinions worth listening to. But he respected me. He believed in me. He saw the best in me. In his company, I began to see all that I could be.'

When we feel wintry because of our personal failures, it might be an idea to imagine a meeting with that woman of the Gospel, and allow her to lead us back down that cicada-singing path to the well of Jacob. There she will tell us about the living waters, the waters for which celebrities and Samaritans alike have longed. These are the wells where we can discover that there are no failures from which we can't recover in this life. The streams of living water are available to all.

Reflection

How can your failures help you discover all that you can be in this life?

Prayer

Lord, when I am wearied with my failures, lead me to the well of living water, that I may become all that I can be in this life.

CONFUSION – THE DISCOVERY OF LIGHT

> Now there was a Pharisee named Nicodemus, a leader of the Jews. He came to Jesus by night and said to him, 'Rabbi, we know that you are a teacher who has come from God; for no one can do these signs that you do apart from the presence of God.' Jesus answered him, 'Very truly, I tell you, no one can see the kingdom of God without being born from above. Nicodemus said to him, 'How can anyone be born after having grown old? Can one enter a second time into the mother's womb and be born?' Jesus answered, 'Very truly, I tell you, no one can enter the kingdom of God without being born of water and Spirit. What is born of the flesh is flesh, and what is born of the Spirit is spirit. Do not be astonished that I said to you, "You must be born from above." The wind blows where it chooses, and you hear the sound of it, but you do not know where it comes from or where it goes. So it is with everyone who is born of the Spirit.'
>
> JOHN 3:1–8 (see also JOHN 3:9–21; 7:45–52; 19:38–42)

Generally, Pharisees get a pretty bad press in the Gospels. Both John the Baptist and Jesus seldom have a good thing to say about them. John the Baptist reckoned they were not much better than a 'brood of vipers'[21] and Jesus accused them of being 'whitewashed tombs... full of the bones of the dead and of all kinds of filth'.[22] The Pharisees were also fairly scathing about Jesus, accusing him, among other things, of being inspired by the devil.[23] In all the Gospels, the Pharisees are people who come over as 'holier than thou', and who enforce many religious burdens on the people. They saw Jesus as being far too cavalier with their well-polished rules, and dangerously subversive.

So when one Pharisee makes his way to Jesus, not to castigate him for his heretical ways but to genuinely engage in a serious conversation, it comes as quite a surprise. The Pharisee in question is a man called Nicodemus. John, our storyteller, tells us that Nicodemus comes to Jesus by night. All references to night and day, dark and light, are significant for John, who proclaims Jesus as a light that has the power to shine in every darkness this world has to offer.[24] Jesus is staying somewhere in Jerusalem during the great feast of Passover, probably with friends. I imagine him sitting out in the courtyard in the cool of the day.

There is a knock at the gate and the person who goes to answer is surprised to see a Pharisee. He says he understands Jesus is stopping at this house. Jesus hears and beckons him to come and sit with him in the bright moonlight. Someone brings the visitor a cup of wine, which he gratefully receives. He sits down awkwardly next to Jesus. His fulsome beard is mostly grey, though still dark over the mouth. His eyebrows are also dark, while the searching eyes beneath them work hard to focus on this rabbi from Galilee.

His voice is kindly as he offers his opening remarks which are conciliatory, almost flattering. Before he has a chance to complete his prepared speech, Jesus interrupts by saying, 'The only way you can see the kingdom of God is by being born all over again.' Nicodemus rocks back on the bench looking startled. What an extraordinary notion! How can anyone possibly return to the womb? It's ludicrous! And yet something about this image of being born over again rings true in the heart of the old Pharisee. So much of his life has not worked out as he hoped. If he could be given the chance to start again, what a lot he would do! He would live with more daring, more adventure. He would not allow himself to be trapped in the doctrines and dogmas that so often have weighed him down.

Both men are quiet for a few moments. The sounds of chatter and laughter rise from the surrounding homes. The conversation has hardly begun, but that one remark from Jesus has highlighted the disturbance that has been in Nicodemus for so long. How does he know who to believe nowadays? This Sadducee? That Pharisee? This scribe? That rabbi? And is all this God-business real anyway? Are they all just fooling themselves, inventing the whole thing from scraps of stories from years gone by? How do you know what to believe about life? About God? About yourself? A breeze spins some dust in front of them and a shutter bangs, rousing Nicodemus from his thoughts.

'Feel that breeze,' says Jesus. 'Where has it come from? And where is it off to? No one knows – it is unseen, but you *feel* it. It even makes the dust dance. Be born of this Spirit, Nicodemus, and so much will start to dance within you. It is not too late.' Nicodemus thinks of the book of Genesis. He is like Adam, made by the hand of God from the dust of the earth. Like Adam, he too can inhale the breath of God, yet he feels that for all of his days the air around him has been stuffy and stale.

Someone comes out into the courtyard with an oil lamp, cupping their hand around the flame. They place it on a stool next to the visitor, who stares at the strong flame that brightens their side of the courtyard. 'Light has come into the world, Nicodemus,' says Jesus, 'and when you find that light, step into it. Too many people want to live in darkness, but you were made for the light.' Nicodemus keeps his eye fixed on the quivering flame and hears himself saying, 'Yes. It's time for the light.' He turns and studies the face of Jesus and knows if there is anywhere in this world where true light can be found, it is in that face. In these moments, in this courtyard, in this breeze, with this man, Nicodemus finally feels a sense of peace. The door is prised open. A part of him locked away for too long is on its way out. Like a newborn babe, he breathes in life-giving air. He feels alive.

John, the writer of our story, never tells us what happens at the end of this conversation. But it is not the last appearance of Nicodemus in his book, for he appears again towards the end. The darkest day in John's story is the day when the light of the life of Jesus is extinguished on the hill of Calvary. It was Nicodemus, together with Joseph of Arimathea, who took the lifeless body of Jesus to the tomb.

None of the disciples were anywhere to be seen in those fatal hours. From somewhere, Nicodemus had collected 75 pounds of myrrh and aloes for the burial – a huge amount normally used for royal burials. As he placed those fragrant spices in the folds of the burial shroud of the one who told him to be born again, what went through the mind of Nicodemus? The very fact that he was there and that he provided such an abundance of spices suggests that by this stage he loved Jesus very deeply. It is perhaps ironic that the one that he was laying in a burial chamber was the one who spoke to him about birth and life. Nicodemus' grief must have been severe. But it is equally likely that in those eventful days following the dramatic resurrection from that tomb, the risen Jesus made a visit to Nicodemus.[25] It was then that Nicodemus discovered what true light is really made of.

We hear no more of Nicodemus after this, but the likelihood is that he often spoke of the light and the wind and new birth. There are times in life when our minds and hearts feel congested with confusion and that can feel like a stuffy, wintry darkness. We seem to lose our ability to make decisions and work out what's right and wrong any more. In such seasons of the soul, it is no bad thing to give thought to this fascinating Pharisee who came to Jesus by night and discovered the light. If we will sit down with him, almost certainly he will say that being born again is not as hard as it seems. It's all about being open and letting the free Spirit of God lead us into new places. In the end, it is about trust, the instinctive gift of the newborn infant.

Reflection

When you feel confused, spend time with this story.

Prayer

Jesus, settle in the courtyards of my confusion, and spark new life in me.

DEPRESSION – THE DISCOVERY OF INSIGHT

[Elijah] sat down under a solitary broom tree. He asked that he might die: 'It is enough; now, O Lord, take away my life, for I am no better than my ancestors.' Then he lay down under the broom tree and fell asleep. Suddenly an angel touched him and said to him, 'Get up and eat.' He looked, and there at his head was a cake baked on hot stones, and a jar of water. He ate and drank, and lay down again. The angel of the Lord came a second time, touched him, and said, 'Get up and eat, otherwise the journey will be too much for you.' He got up, and ate and drank; then he went in the strength of that food for forty days and forty nights to Horeb the mount of God. At that place he came to a cave, and spent the night there.

Then the word of the Lord came to him, saying, 'What are you doing here, Elijah?' He answered, 'I have been very zealous for the Lord, the God of hosts; for the Israelites have forsaken your covenant, thrown down your altars, and killed your prophets with the sword. I alone am left, and they are seeking my life, to take it away.'

He said, 'Go out and stand on the mountain before the Lord, for the Lord is about to pass by.' Now there was a great wind, so strong that it was splitting mountains and breaking rocks in pieces before the Lord, but the Lord was not in the wind; and after the wind an earthquake, but the Lord was not in the earthquake; and after the earthquake a fire, but the Lord was not in the fire; and after the fire a sound of sheer silence. When Elijah heard it, he wrapped his face in his mantle and went out and stood at the entrance of the cave.

1 KINGS 19:4–13 (see also 1 KINGS 18; 19:13–21; 2 KINGS 2:1–12)

Look up the word 'depression' in any dictionary and you will meet words such as 'sadness', 'gloom' and 'dejection'. Your dictionary may also attempt to define the meaning of the word as it is used in the world of psychiatry, and you will probably discover something a good deal more technical. The causes of depression are complex: some relate to events in the here and now; some are due to our past; and some causes are due to chemical imbalances in the brain. Most humans living in the demanding conditions of this mortal life will know moments when the prevailing mood of our soul is one of sadness and despair, and for some people, such a mood can be so intense that it drains life of colour, even of meaning.

Some people of faith work with the naïve supposition that, once you have decided to follow God in your life, such dark valleys of the emotions will be a thing of the past. It can therefore be a rude shock when, despite your radiant faith, you discover an unwelcome pool of gloom lying heavy in your soul. For Christians who follow a Christ who has risen from the dark valley of death, it can be a serious shock to discover that they are dwelling in a land that is more akin to the dark hill of Golgotha, rather than the sunrise garden of the empty tomb. For a number, this is enough to cause their faith to falter. When this is the case, they are in good company: the mighty prophet Elijah was one such person.

We go back to the days of the kings of Israel and Judah who succeeded David and Solomon. It has to be said that they were a pretty rum bunch that, between them, made every mistake in the book and eventually succeeded in losing their lands to the neighbouring powers that overwhelmed them. The main rule they were given was to follow the ways of God and he in turn would bless and protect the people. It sounded simple enough, but it seemed a nigh impossible task for a succession of high-minded men who loved power, and resented God and his prophets telling them what to do. There were of course a few exceptions, but by and large the royal line failed to impress. And there were one or two that were particularly unimpressive, including King Ahab, who was married to the notorious Jezebel.

For a people rooted in devotion to a God they called 'Yahweh', the worst crime was to worship other gods. The most notorious opposing god at the time was 'Baal', and both Ahab and Jezebel expressed a surprising fondness for this disreputable deity. It was soon clear that they were on a collision course with the prophet Elijah, whom Ahab called 'the troubler of Israel'.[26] It all comes to a head in the mighty contest on the top of Mount Carmel.[27] Elijah is triumphant in this contest, and not only manages to draw fire from heaven to burn up a drenched sacrifice, but also slaughters several hundred heretical prophets, brings an end to a three-year drought through his intercessions and, just for good measure, managed to out-sprint Ahab's speeding chariot on his way home.[28]

You would think that nothing could dishearten Elijah after such a successful day's work in which the power of God was evidenced in such unmistakable ways. But you would be wrong. When he hears news that Jezebel is still on the warpath, he hits a pocket of human frailty and is besieged by fear. Close to complete exhaustion, he drags himself off into the wilderness, the only terrain that will do for his tired soul. He has tried his very best, but it seems nothing will shift Ahab and Jezebel from their evil ways, and he feels a dreadful failure. He slumps beneath a broom tree, longing for an end to it all. A kindly angel helps him get going again, and eventually he stumbles his way to a cave on Mount Horeb, and this is where we find this beleaguered prophet.

He is in a restless, dreamless sleep beneath his cloak in the corner of the cave. Scenes of Mount Carmel still visit his mind, but such great events seem so pointless now. He wakes to the sound of a voice. It is a voice that he has learned to trust, and he knows it is a voice of deep love. But it is a voice that too often asks the most disturbing questions, and this one is no exception: 'What are you doing here, Elijah?' It is the question that so deeply haunts him. What on earth *is* he doing here? What is he doing with this life he has been given? What is he doing with his prophetic gifts that may have produced some spectacular displays, yet seemed to have achieved little of real substance? He hardly knows what to say to the question, and the rather feeble reply that eventually falls from his tired lips reveals his loneliness.

The voice seems to ignore his rather plaintive response and tells him to get up and stand at the entrance to the cave. And there he is at the mouth of his cave, high up on the rocky slopes of this mountain of God. Suddenly an immense gust of wind rages past his cave, wrenching lumps of rock from the mountainside and hurling them to the valley below. Never has he experienced such a force of wind as this, but despite the immensity of the power, there is no sign of God in it.

As the wind subsides, he feels the floor of his cave start to vibrate and shift violently. He looks fearfully above him, anxious that the roof of the cave will tumble upon him. On the earthquake goes, shaking the whole vast mountain, and yet one thing remains clear: God is not in the earthquake.

As the earth settles, he then hears the unmistakable roar of a fire, and a moving inferno explodes by the entrance to his cave, causing him to stagger back from its fierce heat. As quickly as it starts, it finishes, and all that is left are the smoking embers of the little shrubs that once clung to the rocks. But again the prophet knows only too clearly: God is not in this fire. So just where is he, this mysterious, puzzling God who once specialised in manifesting himself in the dramatic and miraculous?

And then Elijah experiences something he has never known: absolute, stunning, awesome silence. It fills his cave, the great mountain and the deep valley beneath him. Everything has come to a halt both in the outer world of this wild mountain place, and in the inner world of Elijah's tormented soul. And it is in this silence that Elijah detects the secret, holy presence of God. The prophet of Yahweh stands so still that he could almost be a carved statue at the mouth of this smouldering cave. He has discovered a new side of God that is as still and solid as this ancient mountain. It is in this place of silence that he receives his new call, and a new future opens up. Energy returns to this prophet of the quiet.

Nobody welcomes having to pass through a season of dark depression. But it is comforting to know that even the great prophets of God knew such times. Elijah shows us that beneath the apparent wintry lifeless earth of human depression, something of life is going on. God was with Elijah in the form of the angel to give him the sustenance he needed for his trek through that wilderness, and God still uses all sorts of angels to give us what we need for each stage of our journey. And then there comes the point of listening and true hearing. Often the message is about letting go of old securities, and creating space and stillness to discover new things about God, and indeed about ourselves. Such insights about God, our world, and the lives we are called to live often give new vitality for the journey ahead.

Reflection

Listen in the stillness. What insights are you discovering?

Prayer

When I find myself in wintry, wilderness places, help me, dear Lord, to discover your personal word to me.

CRISIS – THE DISCOVERY OF PRESENCE

Then the king gave the command, and Daniel was brought and thrown into the den of lions. The king said to Daniel, 'May your God, whom you faithfully serve, deliver you!' A stone was brought and laid on the mouth of the den, and the king sealed it with his own signet and with the signet of his lords, so that nothing might be changed concerning Daniel. Then the king went to his palace and spent the night fasting; no food was brought to him, and sleep fled from him.

Then, at break of day, the king got up and hurried to the den of lions. When he came near the den where Daniel was, he cried out anxiously to Daniel, 'O Daniel, servant of the living God, has your God whom you faithfully serve been able to deliver you from the lions?' Daniel then said to the king, 'O king, live for ever! My God sent his angel and shut the lions' mouths so that they would not hurt me, because I was found blameless before him; and also before you, O king, I have done no wrong.' Then the king was exceedingly glad and commanded that Daniel be taken up out of the den. So Daniel was taken up out of the den, and no kind of harm was found on him, because he had trusted in his God.

DANIEL 6:16–23 (see also all of DANIEL 6)

In recent years, I have visited a couple of the great American national parks and there is one thing of which you are made very aware the moment you enter them: the very real threat of wild animals. In Yellowstone Park, as you drive in through the park gates, you are usually given a handful of papers which include rather unnerving warnings on what to do in the event of a bear attack. As one who was brought up on the idea that Yogi and Boo-Boo were interested in no more than the odd picnic basket, it was a bit sobering to discover that the grizzly bear could view a passing tourist as quite a tasty picnic.

The fear of being attacked by a wild animal is primal, and goes right back to our cave-dwelling ancestors who treated wild beasts with the greatest respect. Perhaps it is this primal fear that makes the well-known story of Daniel in the lion's den so popular. Here is a man in a terrifying situation – trapped in a room with only hungry lions for company. It is the stuff of nightmares.

Daniel was one of those who was marched out of Jerusalem by King Nebuchadnezzar and his troops in 605AD and forced to live in exile. As it happens, he accommodated himself quite well to the new and alien culture and managed to gain favour with the king, much to the annoyance of local officials who didn't take kindly to this foreigner gaining such influence, and who resented the fact that he would not give up his faith in God. When a new king called Darius came to the throne in the region, the local satraps saw their chance. Noting the king was a little vulnerable to the lure of vanity, they suggested to him that it might be an idea to encourage all the people of the land to have a period of prayer and devotion that was focused on none other than the fine and magnificent Darius. The conceited king took to this idea, and the satraps recommended that any offender offering prayers to other deities should be thrown into the den of lions. The king obligingly agreed. All around the kingdom people obediently offered their prayers to a deified Darius – apart from one. That one was Daniel who, on hearing the news, promptly went home, threw open the windows and, facing in the direction of Jerusalem, hollered out his prayers to God. As far as the satraps were concerned, the trap had worked a treat and it wasn't long before they were hauling him before King Darius, who had no choice but to condemn Daniel to death by lion.

So we come into this story and see Daniel in the rough hands of his captors. We can see the grim smiles of his tormentors who nod to each other in appreciation of their handiwork. Their nemesis is to be silenced once and for all. The gloss is taken off their delight just a little when the king shows extraordinary respect for Daniel and even declares a wish that the God the satraps are trying so hard to dethrone would actually come to Daniel's rescue.

Quite what an ancient lion den looked like is hard to say. I imagine the entrance to be in the roof of this fearful chamber. A couple of strong men heave at the great stone that covers the roof entrance. As the pit below is revealed, you are hit by the sour smell of animal urine. As you dare glance in, you can see a few chewed bones that glisten in the shafts of sun that break into the dark den. You can hear the sound of quiet paws padding around. Everyone instinctively draws back when they hear the feral growl from the gruesome occupants.

The only person who does not reveal signs of horror is the very person who is about to be lowered into this pit. Daniel has his eyes closed and he is breathing deeply. He is about to face a horrifying death, yet he is utterly serene. In he goes and the king tells the men to pull back the great stone straight away, as he can't bear to hear Daniel's screams that surely will sear at his conscience all too soon. The stone is hauled back over the entrance and the conniving satraps smile contentedly and head off for a celebratory drink.

Inside the pit it is as dark as death, but in a few moments Daniel's eyes adjust, helped by little chinks of light that filter into this cell. He stands still beneath the opening through which he was lowered. He hears the lions growling at the new occupant of their cell. A deep instinct in Daniel, deeper even than the primal fear of the wild creatures, tells him he is safe, and he knows why. There is a presence in this cell, and it is angelic. It is a power stronger than any beast. Every time one of the lions comes close to Daniel, he sees its head drawn away by an unknown force. He kneels in thanksgiving, and then settles down for a good night's sleep – him, the lions and the angel, all resting in peace.

In the morning Darius races to what he imagines will be a tomb of death, and though it seems absurd to imagine Daniel is still alive, he nonetheless cries out to him and is stunned to hear a calm voice reply from the cell below him. Immediately he calls for the stone to be shifted from the opening, and a completely unmolested Daniel is hauled up into the warmth of the rising sun.

Darius doesn't know much about Daniel's God, but he is in no doubt that it is this God who has saved him. It may even have crossed his mind that if this is part of what gods have to do, he would be better off returning to being a mere mortal as soon as possible.

The lions' den story is the end of the first part of the Daniel book. The chapters that follow are mostly accounts of extraordinary dreams and visions that Daniel experienced. Scholars have argued for centuries over the meaning of these strange spiritual sightings, but one thing it does tell us is that Daniel had developed a most unusual way of seeing. Dreams that we might write off as the result of too much wine the night before, he respected as having deep significance. He allowed impressions in the mind to develop into full-blown visions. It was perhaps this gift that helped him to see the angel in that lions' den.

Maybe this is the gift of a crisis: it is an opportunity to discover we are not alone. Sometimes we are so focused on the crisis, we fail to notice there are angels all over the place that are heavenly bearers of grace. It might be the random comment of a child; or a rainbow arching across a dark sky; or an unexpected visit of a good friend. It is the testimony of countless people of faith that in times of genuine crisis there has been a sense of presence lifting them out of their fears into a place of peace. Many have testified to seeing visions – glimpses of life that perhaps could not be seen in normal circumstances. In crises, senses can be heightened. We can see and hear things that we overlook when life is going well. In short, we can become very aware of the presence of God.

Thankfully, I never did get on the wrong side of a grizzly bear in those national parks and I have no doubt that if I had, I should have swiftly discovered the meaning of primal fear. However, my experiences of other crises in life have told me that, uncomfortable as they are, these can be seasons of discovery, not least of the presence of God. It seems that some wisdom can only be found in the dark.

Reflection

Think about the crises you have passed through in your life – what discoveries did you make?

Prayer

Lord, when I find myself in the dark den of fear, give me the gift of discerning the presence of your angel messengers of grace.

SPRING

The season
of birthing

INTRODUCTION

'There is no time like spring, when life's alive in everything,' wrote Christina Rosetti in her ebullient poem called 'Spring'. This season is certainly a time of extraordinary vitality. The early Celtic people called it *Imbolc* and it began on 1 February. In my experience in Britain, February can still be a pretty cold month, and we are by no means clear of ice, frost and snow. But there is no denying the signs of new life at this time as bold shoots of bulbs push their heads through cold earth. Snowdrops, crocuses, anemones and daffodils brighten the land whose colours were muted during the winter season. And it is during February that we start to notice the light returning, and by the time we get into March the rate of change speeds up and we notice the lighter mornings and evenings. Come April, we see the bright, vivid greens being established in the countryside, and although it is sometimes reluctant to do so, the cold north wind gives way to warmer breezes from the west and south. Nothing beats those days when we step outside and feel the warmth of the sun on our faces and many think or say words to the effect of, 'Welcome back, dear sun – how we have missed you!'

There is a most delightful poem on spring in the book called 'The Song of Songs'. This book is a lavish love song traditionally connected with the great King Solomon. It has caused some anxiety to those down the ages who have been nervous of sexual references in the Bible. But the references are there for all to see whether they like it or not. It is a book that is unashamedly taking delight in the love between man and woman. In chapter 2 of this beautiful book, we read a passage that in some versions of the Bible is called the 'Springtime Rhapsody' and it includes these words,

My beloved speaks and says to me:
'Arise, my love, my fair one,
   and come away;
for now the winter is past,
   the rain is over and gone.
The flowers appear on the earth;
   the time of singing has come,
and the voice of the turtle-dove
   is heard in our land.
The fig tree puts forth its figs,
   and the vines are in blossom;
   they give forth fragrance.
Arise, my love, my fair one,
   and come away.[29]

The writer of Song of Songs clearly saw a strong connection between the birthing of this romantic love with the new life that so evidently erupts in our greening springtime. Spring is the season of birthing – the earth, which seemed so dormant and barren only a few weeks before, is now delivering an apparently endless flow of life into the brightening world. In the journey of the soul, springtimes come as we make new discoveries, and things are birthed in us that surprise and delight us. But glorious as these new births may be, they can also bring their own fair share of disturbance and challenge, as we shall see in the stories that follow.

INFANT –
BIRTHING NEW LIFE

Hannah rose and presented herself before the Lord. Now Eli the priest was sitting on the seat beside the doorpost of the temple of the Lord. She was deeply distressed and prayed to the Lord, and wept bitterly. She made this vow: 'O Lord of hosts, if only you will look on the misery of your servant, and remember me, and not forget your servant, but will give to your servant a male child, then I will set him before you as a nazirite until the day of his death. He shall drink neither wine nor intoxicants, and no razor shall touch his head...'

Then the woman went to her quarters, ate and drank with her husband, and her countenance was sad no longer.

They rose early in the morning and worshipped before the Lord; then they went back to their house at Ramah. Elkanah knew his wife Hannah, and the Lord remembered her. In due time Hannah conceived and bore a son. She named him Samuel, for she said, 'I have asked him of the Lord.'

1 SAMUEL 1:9–11, 18–20 (see also all of 1 SAMUEL 1; 1 SAMUEL 2:1–11)

The story of Hannah is set over 1,000 years before Christ, in the days when the Hebrew people had settled into their promised land, but were in need of wise leadership. Hannah is someone who gives birth to one of their great leaders.

Her story is so beautifully written that it is not difficult to imagine the scene. I see her as if she were the subject of a Rembrandt painting: she is seated on a wooden stool in the doorway to her simple dwelling. The rays of the early morning sun spread warm light on her as she looks out to the hills beyond her village. Everything behind her is painted in dark shadowy tones. As was the custom of the time, Elkanah had another wife. She is called Peninnah, and she, Elkanah and the children are sound asleep in the dark background. But Hannah is vividly awake, because something wonderful has happened. For too long she has been childless and the subject of much taunting by Peninnah. So she went up to the house of the Lord and offloaded before God her grief and pain at her childless state. She was so beside herself with anguish that old Eli, the priest, thought she was drunk on wine.

Several weeks had now passed since that time of intense prayer, and remarkably there was no sign of the monthly losses of blood that had become grim reminders of the loss of hope from her heart. As each day went by, she dared to believe that she really was nursing a new life within her. On this morning, as I imagine it, she was awoken from her sleep by a movement from deep within her. There could be no doubt about it. The stirring, though tiny, was definitely there. She was with child and this child was moving and making his presence known. The Lord had heard her desperate prayer, and now she sits there in that doorway, the sun streaming on her upturned face, and her hand stroking her belly, within which the tiny life resides.

It is, at one level, such a human story. Anyone who has known childlessness, or been close to someone who has experienced this, knows how acute this pain can be. Occasionally for some people, that pain has found dramatic healing with a much longed-for pregnancy and new life. These experiences remind us that all life is a miracle and gift. For many of those who do become parents, when they welcome their newborn child into their arms for the first time, they feel a keen sense of the holy, the miraculous, the presence of God. It is such a mystery, and way beyond human comprehension. If you are reading this today nursing a newborn, or close to someone who is, you may be feeling something of this. A precious infant has been entrusted to you, to nurture and care for her or him and guide them through the complex world into which they have been born.

It is such a high calling that it is not surprising that many people who would never normally darken the door of a church nonetheless make their way there with their newborn with an instinctive desire to give thanks and seek a blessing. They know that this gift is more than they could produce by themselves and, so precious is the gift, they must find a way of giving thanks and asking a blessing from heaven on this precious new life. Hence every Sunday there are baptisms and dedications in churches all over the world.

In the story of Hannah, we discover that her baby boy had an unusual and particular calling on his life, and he grew up to play a very significant role as a leader of the people of Israel. Because she was so deeply prayerful, Hannah had insight into this right from the moment she became pregnant. Only a handful of babies born today will become famous in their time. But every child born today has a destiny and calling. Parents can follow the example of Hannah and listen to God for their child, before birth, and through their early years. We may only hear snippets of the story, but those snippets can help us to direct them into the pathways where they will flourish and become all that they can be in this world.

The gift of a new life always has a springtime feel about it. Hannah's prayer of thanksgiving in 1 Samuel 2:1–10 is full of spring-like joy. That is not to say that it is a spring without a few cold winds. Disturbed nights, endless nappies, unwanted depression and stresses of many kinds can rob us of the initial joy. But most parents find that, notwithstanding the many stresses, when they lay their child down in the evening, they can sit and gaze at their infant child in such a way that they lose all sense of time and space.

This story of new life has a slightly bittersweet ending because Hannah feels called to 'give her son to the Lord' (v. 28). As soon as he was weaned she took him to the house of the Lord at Shiloh. Whatever we may think of this, we can see in Hannah a deep conviction that all life is a gift not to be grasped at and hoarded, but to be shared with others. All parents sense this as their children grow up – as the years go by they make their own way in the world. This is the nature of new life – it is never to be possessed, but to be shared with others.

Reflection

If you have recently had a child join your family or circle of friends, spend a few moments in deep listening and see if you can discern something about this child's destiny.

Prayer

Creator God, when I catch sight of a newborn, open my eyes and heart to the wonder of new life.

CREATION –
BIRTHING WONDER

In the day that the Lord God made the earth and the heavens, when no plant of the field was yet in the earth and no herb of the field had yet sprung up – for the Lord God had not caused it to rain upon the earth, and there was no one to till the ground; but a stream would rise from the earth, and water the whole face of the ground – then the Lord God formed man from the dust of the ground, and breathed into his nostrils the breath of life; and the man became a living being. And the Lord God planted a garden in Eden, in the east; and there he put the man whom he had formed. Out of the ground the Lord God made to grow every tree that is pleasant to the sight and good for food, the tree of life also in the midst of the garden, and the tree of the knowledge of good and evil.

GENESIS 2:4–9 (see also GENESIS 1)

If it were possible to flag down the Doctor from *Doctor Who* and hitch a lift in his TARDIS, it would be very interesting to set his satnav to transport us to the creation of all things. I suppose it would settle a few issues about how this planet came into being. We could take our phones and capture some good shots of it all. The panoramic setting would work nicely. We could attempt a few movies as well. Then the good Doctor would speed us home and we could certainly fill a few lecture halls, giving fascinating talks with thrilling PowerPoint slides and film clips. The creationists would be there – those who hold to a literal understanding of a seven-day creation. They would be hoping we had set the date and time on our phones. The scientists would turn up too, checking out if their favoured theories would still hold water. Geologists would be immensely keen to see if we had managed to fetch a few rock samples while we were there. We would certainly be popular and not be short of work for quite a few years.

Just trying to imagine such a scenario illustrates how impossible the task is. We are talking about the beginning of this bright, spinning globe that, against unimaginable odds, became a habitable home for human life. Anyone trying to write about the commencement of this remarkable world in the immensity of this universe is almost doomed to failure – except that a couple of writers have all but managed it. Who they were, we don't really know, but some people wrote the first pages of the Bible in the book that came to be called Genesis. We see two accounts of creation in chapters 1 and 2, almost certainly written by two different writers from different times in history. It is clear from the way they write that they were poet storytellers, and poets write from and for the heart. They are inclined to be a little impatient with scientists. Scientists struggle with poets and run into trouble if they take them too literally.

These poets listened intently and, after listening, they wrote down what they heard. They listened to a trail of ancient wisdom that went back down the generations. They put those stories alongside their own experience. They were people who harkened to their world. They would go to the hilltop at the end of the day and watch the burning sun settle gently behind the dark mountains. They would wait until little specks of sparkling light glimmered in the darkening sky, and watch the mottled moon turn the landscape silver. They observed. They wondered. They prayed. They listened to God's creative Spirit. What went through the minds of those ancient people? Whatever it was, we can glean from these intriguing early stories in Genesis that they held a profound wonder at the created order. They saw everything as part of a God-blessed harmony of water, earth, light, dark, mountain, plain, tree, plant, insect, animal – everything. In origin and in essence, this created planet was *good* and it was called into being by a good God.

The creation stories describe to us a world where humans and nature live in a precious harmony. Why, even the man is formed from the very dust of the earth. There is a blessed interdependence. We were made to belong to each other. The earth is a true home where humans can flourish and walk with their God in the cool of the day.

Of course the poets spotted the tree in the garden and it certainly put a stutter in their cadences. They had seen it again and again – humans glancing up at forbidden fruit while the devious words of a tempter slithered into their ear, promising so much yet at such cost. Whatever you make of that story of Adam and Eve and forbidden fruit (Genesis 3), the message that those poets professed loud and clear was that when humans mess things up, their relationship with the earth suffers. These poets had seen such things even in their own souls. The experience of Eden is with us every day. We have the choice – to live in wonder, generosity and care, or to grasp for that which is not ours and thereby darken the world for others.

Those two Genesis poets lived a long time before the eco-warriors, but they clearly had something of their passion, and it is their passion we need to listen out for as we read these well-known accounts of creation. To read these stories in order to learn scientific facts or win theological contests is to miss the point. Those writers wanted us to get ourselves into these stories and feel our way around in them. 'Come in and join us,' we can hear them saying today. 'Come and feel the softness of the new unpoisoned soil. Come, listen to the sound of the rising lark, unimpaired by the roar of the motorway. Come close and stroke the mane of the noble lion in the world where he knows no enmity with you. Come, feel your instinct, your longing, your yearning for paradise. Come, see the earth as it was always meant to be. Feel the tears in your eyes as you imagine such things. Listen to your tears, your laughter, your longings as you survey such wonders.'

When it comes to the environment, we have almost become immune to the endless reports, warnings and predictions of catastrophe. However, a moment with the poets of Genesis feels different. Step into those chapters with open eyes and heart, and see what the sheer wonder of God's precious gift of this earth might evoke in you. You don't need a TARDIS – you need a soul that is willing to let the Spirit of God breathe upon it. 'Then God said, "Let there be light"; and there was light. And God saw that the light was good.'[30] This good light will always work its wonders.

Reflection

Spend time in Genesis chapters 1 and 2. Imagine yourself in this early world and listen to what is evoked in you.

Prayer

My Creator God, grant me the eyes to see the true wonders of this world you have crafted for all humankind.

ADVENTURE – BIRTHING VISION

Now the Lord said to Abram, 'Go from your country and your kindred and your father's house to the land that I will show you. I will make of you a great nation, and I will bless you, and make your name great, so that you will be a blessing. I will bless those who bless you, and the one who curses you I will curse; and in you all the families of the earth shall be blessed.'

So Abram went, as the Lord had told him; and Lot went with him. Abram was seventy-five years old when he departed from Haran. Abram took his wife Sarai and his brother's son Lot, and all the possessions that they had gathered, and the persons whom they had acquired in Haran; and they set forth to go to the land of Canaan. When they had come to the land of Canaan, Abram passed through the land to the place at Shechem, to the oak of Moreh. At that time the Canaanites were in the land. Then the Lord appeared to Abram, and said, 'To your offspring I will give this land.' So he built there an altar to the Lord, who had appeared to him. From there he moved on to the hill country on the east of Bethel, and pitched his tent, with Bethel on the west and Ai on the east; and there he built an altar to the Lord and invoked the name of the Lord. And Abram journeyed on by stages towards the Negeb.

GENESIS 12:1–9

Abram has just enjoyed a good supper of roast goat and vegetables. His elderly wife is clattering away in their simple kitchen, though with her poor eyesight and the failing light, she is not making a great job of cleaning the dishes. Abram finds his favourite spot in the garden and settles into a seat that is so used to his frame that it has become moulded to his shape. This is his evening chair, where he can lean back and gaze up at the glittering night sky. He lifts his tired legs to a stool and his eyes to the night sky and watches a dazzling meteor speed towards the horizon. His neighbour's chickens chunter away to themselves as they gather into a shelter for the night. Abram is content and safe. Yet something is restless within him. As he drifts into his post-dinner nap, the sound of those chickens is replaced by another noise that sounds remarkably like a voice. The voice gets clearer and clearer, and though Abram is asleep, he is also extraordinarily awake. More awake than he has ever been. And the voice speaks to him: 'Go from your country and your kindred and your father's house to the land that I will show you.'

We don't know too much about Abram before this bit of the story. His father Terah was the first to get itchy feet: he had set out from Ur of the Chaldees in the hopes of getting to Canaan, but had stalled at Haran and eventually died there. So was it that Abram inherited this restless yearning and was looking to get going again on the adventure to Canaan? Or had he decided that it was no more than a bright idea of his father's? Well, either way, he nonetheless got a very specific message from God to don his boots and get a move on.

So up Abram gets from his comfy garden chair and takes one last look at the night sky before he gets on with his packing. All those stars above shimmer in delight. It won't be long before the Almighty speaks to him about his descendents numbering as many as those stars.[31] The sight of the elderly Abram, Sarai and Lot making their way out of town with their well-laden donkeys must have raised a few eyebrows. However, off they go and the subsequent chapters in Genesis detail for us their adventures, which are considerable. But, despite some alarms and mishaps, they do make it to the promised land and, miraculously Sarai bears a child, and the descendents flourish. Abram opened his heart to new adventures and, though the road he travelled was hazardous, you get the clear impression he never regretted his decision.

Many have used this passage to encourage people in later life to be open to new callings and adventures. I have witnessed many people who, when it comes to the days of checking in for their pensions, have looked up to the heavens for signals, and they have found wonderful new exploits. Like Abram and Sarai, off they have gone, often with doubtful glances from those who judge them too old for such things. But you don't have to be elderly to seek wisdom from the Abram and Sarai story. As it turns out, according to the writer of their story, they were not even halfway through their long lives when they upped sticks and headed for Canaan.

Any of us can get too settled at any stage of our lives. All adventure involves risk – it would not be an adventure without it. Abram's journey was highly risky. But what kept him steady was the sense that it was God who called him on this journey, and his God could be trusted. True, this trust was tested many times; there were a few false starts and wrong turns on the journey. But each time God was there to guide and rescue him.

Abraham (as he came to be called) travelled a most unusual road and his calling involved founding a nation. Few of us feel we nurture quite such exalted vocations, but nonetheless when I read the story of Abraham and Sarah, I feel challenged again to review my life. It is often just when we feel like it is time to settle down that our God can disturb us with a thought dropped into our mind, or a dream in the night, or a book that stirs us, or a chance conversation that opens new possibilities. For many of us, we immediately embark on a mental risk analysis and, before we know it, the door to the adventure is closed. But if we look around at who has changed this broken world for the better, it is so often those who have been willing to open their hearts and minds to a new vision.

The evening before I wrote this, I spotted in the night sky the International Space Station that was hurtling at 17,000 miles an hour through space, 250 miles above my home. It is a bright, steady shooting star, sailing regularly around our spinning world. If

Abraham were alive today, what might he have thought of the sight of it as he pondered the night sky? My guess is that an old adventurer like him would be noting such a journey for his bucket list.

Reflection

What new experience or adventure might God be calling you to?

Prayer

Adventuring God, nurture in me a bold, springtime spirit that is open to catching sight of a new vision and a new journey.

LOVE – BIRTHING ROMANCE

Then Laban said to Jacob, 'Because you are my kinsman, should you therefore serve me for nothing? Tell me, what shall your wages be?' Now Laban had two daughters; the name of the elder was Leah, and the name of the younger was Rachel. Leah's eyes were lovely, and Rachel was graceful and beautiful. Jacob loved Rachel; so he said, 'I will serve you seven years for your younger daughter Rachel.' Laban said, 'It is better that I give her to you than that I should give her to any other man; stay with me.' So Jacob served seven years for Rachel, and they seemed to him but a few days because of the love he had for her.

Then Jacob said to Laban, 'Give me my wife that I may go in to her, for my time is completed.' So Laban gathered together all the people of the place, and made a feast. But in the evening he took his daughter Leah and brought her to Jacob; and he went in to her... When morning came, it was Leah! And Jacob said to Laban, 'What is this you have done to me? Did I not serve with you for Rachel? Why then have you deceived me?' Laban said, 'This is not done in our country – giving the younger before the firstborn. Complete the week of this one, and we will give you the other also in return for serving me for another seven years.' Jacob did so, and completed her week; then Laban gave him his daughter Rachel as a wife. (Laban gave his maid Bilhah to his daughter Rachel to be her maid.) So Jacob went in to Rachel also, and he loved Rachel more than Leah. He served Laban for another seven years.

GENESIS 29:15–30 (see also GENESIS 27:41—28:5; 29:1–14)

Jacob is a young man on the run from his raging twin brother, Esau. They had an edgy relationship even before they were born and Jacob pushed his luck too far when he succeeded in deceiving his elderly father, Isaac, into giving him a birthright that belonged to Esau. Their mother, Rebekah, favoured Jacob and played no small part in the deceit. When she realised just how wild with fury Esau had become on discovering the ill-fated plot, she advised Jacob to pack his bags and flee to Laban, Rebekah's brother, who lived a safe distance away in a place called Haran.

So Jacob goes, leaving behind him his home, family and all the dreams he had of living from the good of his father's blessing. He is the grandson of the great Abraham, and everyone had such high hopes for him. But now he is a fugitive far from home. However, when he is within striking distance of Haran, he stops for a rest by a well and meets some men who know his uncle Laban. But more importantly, as he sits by the well enjoying some cool water, someone else comes along. She is beautiful, and Jacob's heart is immediately lost to her. In those days being a first cousin was no prohibition to marriage, so as soon as he gets an opportunity, he asks Laban for her hand in marriage. This is where the love story gets a little more complicated, because Laban is a shrewd and somewhat callous businessman. He spots an opportunity to get seven years' good service out of this nephew and he does a deal with him. The writer of our story tells us that such was the depth of Jacob's love for his girl that these seven years seemed like days.

The wedding day arrives, and the devious Laban spots an opportunity to wring a further seven years out of his nephew and puts the older daughter, Leah, under a heavy veil for the wedding. Somehow or other, Jacob never spots the deception until the morning after where he realises it is Leah, not Rachel, in his wedding bed.

Perhaps we can imagine the scene of that morning. I see Jacob by a simple yet sturdy gate at the edge of the farmstead. He leans on the gate, clasping his hands together that have been hardened by seven years of labouring on this farm. His eyes look piercingly into the long distance over the rough, dry plain. He is almost motionless apart from a regular twitching of his jawbone that betrays his clenched teeth and inner fury. He has just come from a stormy meeting with Laban. He has been deceived and even he might have recognised the irony; he has done his fair share of deceiving and here he is getting his comeuppance. He took the hand he believed belonged to his sweet beloved, only to find it was her sister's. In his bed now lay Leah, contented in her newly married state. Somewhere else was Rachel, alone and in shock. Her own father had tricked the man she so deeply cherished. The wedding celebration was to be the summit of their love, but it turned out to be a pit of despair.

And yet, all is by no means lost. Thankfully even Laban recognises true love when he sees it. He knows he cannot keep these two apart for long. He has got what he wanted – both daughters betrothed, and another seven years' hard labour from this sturdy nephew. Jacob stands up stiffly and grips the crossbar of the gate with his firm fists. He looks up to the sky but closes his eyes against the bright sun that now beams upon him. A week – that is all Laban has asked. A week with Leah, and then it will be Rachel. In the days when more than one wife was allowed, this did not present too much of a problem. The sense of betrayal and shock slips from him, dispersing like the morning mist that is thinning over the nearby river. As the sun warms his tired eyes, he imagines the glowing smile of his beloved. Bitterness is thawing under the beams of radiant love. What are seven years of hard labour in this world when love lightens the heart? He turns from his station at the gate. He is ready now to find Rachel. Their story of love has been challenged, but in the end it is their love, not Laban's deception, that has triumphed.

This well-known love story in the book of Genesis is one that still touches us. Those who have known what it is to fall in love read this story with understanding. They have no problem seeing how Jacob endured the hardships laid on him by Laban. They know that, to use the language of the Song of Songs, 'many waters cannot quench love, neither can floods drown it'.[32] The strength of this kind of love is truly extraordinary.

But such love does not mean that life becomes easy, nor that the love will be without its times of testing. For Jacob, this love story caused him to face his own patterns of woundedness. He had deceived his father and his brother, and now here he is, deceived by his father-in-law. To step into the world of love can expose all kinds of weaknesses that were once safely hidden. There is a sense that we become less defended when we are in love. The harsh parts of our world can feel more abrasive, because our inner skin has become so much more tender. Being in a loving relationship of this kind is both a wonder and a disturbance. The season is most certainly that springtime described so beautifully in the Song of Songs. But even the best of springs can have their stormy and frosty days. On such days it would be good to go and knock on Jacob's door, and there we would find him clasping the hand of a smiling Rachel. Then he might look at us with a sparkle in his eye and ask, 'What storm? What frost? What years of labour?' It would be the way he pulled Rachel to himself and kissed the top of her head that would tell you that true romance is made of a God-blessed love of an indestructible kind.

Reflection

As you reflect on your own experience of romantic love, how has it fared when it has been challenged?

Prayer

Lord, fashion my heart that it may render true love.

CREATIVITY – BIRTHING IMAGINATION

The Lord spoke to Moses: See, I have called by name Bezalel son of Uri son of Hur, of the tribe of Judah: and I have filled him with divine spirit, with ability, intelligence, and knowledge in every kind of craft, to devise artistic designs, to work in gold, silver, and bronze, in cutting stones for setting, and in carving wood, in every kind of craft. Moreover, I have appointed with him Oholiab son of Ahisamach, of the tribe of Dan; and I have given skill to all the skilful, so that they may make all that I have commanded you: the tent of meeting, and the ark of the covenant, and the mercy-seat that is on it, and all the furnishings of the tent, the table and its utensils, and the pure lampstand with all its utensils, and the altar of incense, and the altar of burnt-offering with all its utensils, and the basin with its stand, and the finely worked vestments, the holy vestments for the priest Aaron and the vestments of his sons, for their service as priests, and the anointing-oil and the fragrant incense for the holy place. They shall do just as I have commanded you.

EXODUS 31:1–11 (see also EXODUS 35:25–35)

One of the writers of the creation story wrote that humans are created 'in the image of God'.[33] They had a remarkably positive view of human nature and they were on to a truth that has inspiring implications for humanity. Troubled and fallen though we are as a species, humans are instinctively creative. To be made 'in the image' of God means that there must be something of that creative life in all of us.

There is a rather unsung hero in the Bible who illustrates this beautifully. He appears in those accounts recorded in the book of Exodus of the 40-year wilderness journey of the people of God to the promised land. The gentleman in question is Bezalel, who is in charge of designing and constructing the tabernacle and various accoutrements including the great and sacred ark of the covenant. He is introduced twice in the book of Exodus, in chapters 31 and 35, and several chapters are devoted to his skilful and artistic creations. It makes for fascinating reading as fabrics, colours and dimensions are all recorded in great detail. Suddenly, in the middle of this dull and rather wretched desert, Bezalel organises the construction of something that is exquisitely beautiful. The contrast with the desert surroundings must have been astounding.

You can perhaps imagine Bezalel there on a hot desert day at his makeshift workbench, measuring out a piece of acacia wood. Oholiab, his faithful colleague, is talking to one of the women who has just crafted a most exquisite finely woven indigo drape. Bezalel goes over and strokes the smooth fabric with his rough hands, and sighs in deep contentment. The woman smiles with pride as the master builder praises her handiwork. Not far from him, some men are hauling one of the great outer drapes up to the supporting poles. The tabernacle is taking shape. But Bezalel's mind is now working fast on the greatest work of all – the making of the ark of the covenant, that sacred golden box that will symbolise the near presence of God. What a task to be given!

He steps back from the engrossed workers and walks purposefully out into the shimmering desert to find a quiet spot, where he stands as still as the time-worn rocks around him. He inhales deeply, imagining that he is drawing into his soul a special measure of God's creative Spirit for this task. How does God want this ark to look? God has revealed the design to Moses, but Bezalel needs to imagine it if he is to craft it well. Colours and shapes flood into his fertile mind. The colours settle into a bright burnished gold as he sees in his creative mind's eye the shape of two cherubim, those mighty angelic creatures who worship God day and night in the heavenly places. They are to be represented on this ark of the covenant, kneeling upon it with their magnificent wings gently folded towards the centre, beckoning the people into the presence of their God. He lifts his arms in praise to the God who has allowed him to see such wonders. Bright-eyed, he hurries back to his workbench, his flimsy sandals raising a fine cloud of dust behind him. He finds the goldsmith and tells him the news and they both laugh in delight.

Reading the story of Bezalel again, I am struck by the extraordinary release of fertile creative life in the midst of this barren wasteland. The people donate their precious bits of gold and jewellery, and they also offer their considerable talents. Men and women work together to create a gorgeous work of art in this desert place. When the work was completed, and they all gathered in that tabernacle, and Aaron appeared in all his finery to lead the worship, pretty much every person there would have been able to see the part they had played in creating that grand endeavour. Bezalel would be the first to admit that the influence behind it all was the Holy Spirit of the creator God. It was an unexpected springtime in the desert. The tabernacle that they constructed so beautifully, along with cherubim-covered ark, became a place of deep renewal. It became a place of hope and a place where the presence of God was felt.

It is heartening to read this story of Bezalel, to see how the Spirit of God fired his imagination in such a dramatic way to bring about such infectious creativity in a very unpromising place. The same Spirit is active today. No desert is strong enough to suppress creative life: a Soweto family forms a string quartet and exquisite music resounds from a street of simple shacks; a group of army wives, who feel they can't sing to save their lives, find themselves forming a choir and sing in the Royal Albert Hall before the Queen; a scientist trapped by a paralysing disease stuns the world with his brilliant discoveries. And a multitude of people in everyday lives and of all ages, who thought they were no good at sewing, potting, dancing, writing, painting, music and all other kinds of crafts discover a freedom and confidence that releases their creative skills. A dormant part of them springs to life like the wilderness that blossoms after a shower of rain.

Bezalel would well understand this, for each time he stepped into that holy tabernacle, he knew he was meeting a God who loved to draw springtime, creative life, from the people he had designed in his own image. Too often we close down the creative side of our lives because we fear ridicule or criticism, or because we have been made to feel that our many imperfections will be too much for any image of God to break through. But any of us can have our days, when we can step to one side and catch the eye of Bezalel, who would remind us that the Spirit who ignited that creative life in him is freely available to any of us.

Reflection

What creative gifts are you using? What may lie dormant in you at the moment? What do you need to start using these?

Prayer

Try laying your hand on your mind and praying, 'Come, Holy Spirit of my creator God, release your creative life in my mind today and set my imagination alight.'

HEALING – BIRTHING
NEW WELLBEING

Now [Jesus] was teaching in one of the synagogues on the sabbath. And just then there appeared a woman with a spirit that had crippled her for eighteen years. She was bent over and was quite unable to stand up straight. When Jesus saw her, he called her over and said, 'Woman, you are set free from your ailment.' When he laid his hands on her, immediately she stood up straight and began praising God. But the leader of the synagogue, indignant because Jesus had cured on the sabbath, kept saying to the crowd, 'There are six days on which work ought to be done; come on those days and be cured, and not on the sabbath day.' But the Lord answered him and said, 'You hypocrites! Does not each of you on the sabbath untie his ox or his donkey from the manger, and lead it away to give it water? And ought not this woman, a daughter of Abraham whom Satan bound for eighteen long years, be set free from this bondage on the sabbath day?' When he said this, all his opponents were put to shame; and the entire crowd was rejoicing at all the wonderful things that he was doing.

LUKE 13:10–17

If you have reached wherever you are in life without suffering sickness of one kind or another, you can count yourself very fortunate. Most people are sooner or later hit by some failure in their body or mind, and need the help of the medical and pharmaceutical professions to help them out. Some discover that even these sophisticated resources are not enough to rescue them from their illness and they have to face the prospect of a long-term sickness, and for some this means for the rest of their lives. For the sufferers and carers alike, this can be a very heavy burden to bear. And it is clear that this human experience was no different in the time of Jesus, where so many suffered the distress of long-term illnesses including the whole range of diseases that affected bones and joints that left people crooked and lame.

Luke mentions one such sufferer in his Gospel. She happened to be attending a synagogue one day when Jesus visited. We don't know her name, age or anything about her, save that she suffered from a spinal problem that was clearly evident in her crippled body, and this she had endured for 18 years. Luke tells us that the cause of this problem was a spirit. Theologians, pastors and medics have argued for centuries about quite what this means, but for the woman, the cause of her infirmity was probably the least of her worries, as she had to put all her energies into just getting through each day, not solving theological conundrums. No doubt she also had to manage the bittersweet memories of days gone by when she could walk tall and stretch her head back to gaze at the birds in flight above her and spread her arms freely to the open sky in delight. But now her future was a life trapped in a steadily declining and stooped body. Yet she was there, at the synagogue saying her prayers, and maybe she felt that where there was life there was always hope.

One morning a Nazareth-raised rabbi has come to town and, as it is the sabbath, he makes his way to the synagogue. She has heard news of this man and is not quite sure what to make of him. She has heard that he cures the lame and delivers the oppressed, and she waits in a shadowy corner of the women's section in the synagogue and looks forward to hearing what he has to say. Her bent figure is a good deal smaller than the other women, and her attempts to raise her head to look ahead causes her pain. It is easier to simply look at the dull dusty floorboards of the synagogue. She has become an expert student of floors.

The rabbi from Nazareth is about to speak, but pauses. To the woman's amazement, the people around her are calling her forward.

The rabbi wants to speak to *her*, and, as she cranes her painful neck up, she sees him reaching a hand out to her. She shuffles towards him, terribly aware of the rest of the synagogue falling silent and observing her. This is the last thing she wanted – many of them don't know what to do with someone with her condition and she much prefers to keep herself to herself, apart from a few select friends. But herself now has to be shared in public, and with this teacher called Jesus, whose hand is stretched towards her.

As she reaches him, she limply raises her thin hand towards his and he grasps hold of it, and then he bends down to her level. For a moment it looks like he has the same disease as her. One arm is outstretched to hold her, and the other he rests on his knee, to support himself. He looks firmly into her tired eyes. For years most people have tried to avoid her gaze, but here is someone who wants to look at her eye-to-eye. She strains her neck up a little and looks at the dark eyes that are different to any others she has seen. There is something more in those eyes – a quality that is beholding her in a way that seems to know her. They see more than a crippled woman bent double in a synagogue. It is as if they see her in a different light. She has never seen herself as particularly holy, but something in the hold of the hand and look of the eye of this curious rabbi makes her feel like she wants to dance with the angels.

Those silent moments seem to last for an eternity and, just as the pain in the neck becomes too much to bear, she lowers her head and hears the silence broken by a voice which says so simply and quietly, and yet so directly, 'Dear woman – you are free.' Yes, he is right, in her heart, she is sensing a new freedom. But, wait a minute – there seems to be another freedom. He has let go of her hand, which remains in the same place as if it is still being held. The palms of his hands now press down on her greying head and she feels their warmth. That heat now penetrates into her brain – she feels it like a liquid being poured into her, and down it flows into her brittle and bent backbone, driving out 18 years of pain. She feels that something dark has let go of its grip on her.

The man from Nazareth removes his hands, but the warmth remains. For years it has been too painful to even attempt to straighten her body, but now she does what she has yearned to do for so long: she lifts up her head which in turn draws her backbone up straight and strong. She suddenly sees the world from her full height and looks at people face-to-face. She feels so tall she almost loses her balance. Someone near her starts to laugh nervously – everyone knows she can't do this, and yet she is doing it! A murmuring starts around the room like a rustling breeze in the rafters. Her arms are lifted up – she doesn't remember lifting them but she sees them high above her head and one of her great and loyal friends screams in delight – so undignified in the synagogue! She knows she is cured – there can be no doubt, and as her tears fall to the dry floorboards beneath her she cries out words of praise to her God in heaven. Not only is her body cured, but something has been released in her spirit. She knows she is now liberated and all she wants to do is to thank the one who has rescued her.

While her family and friends flutter around her with hugs and laughter, she hears the voice of the synagogue ruler lodging his complaint about a breach of the sabbath rules. At this moment in time she could not care less about ridiculous sabbath rules – she has met a God who is interested in far more important things than that. Rules be damned! The people have been bent and bowed for too long by such rules. She knows this extraordinary Jesus will now set about another healing, the healing of that ruler's mind which is as crippled by darkness as her body was. But she will leave that to Jesus – she has got some catching up to do.

Miracles were never far away from the ministry of Jesus and, for those religious leaders who liked their religion tidy and nicely controlled, such breaking of normal natural rules was very disturbing. But Jesus' heart was set not on preserving a religious institution, but on freeing humans from their suffering. That woman in our story is one of countless millions down the ages who have found that an unexpected encounter with Jesus has resulted in freedom and healing. For those who have suffered a long winter of sickness, such liberation is a marvellous springtime.

The whole area of divine healing is a mystery, for there are countless people who have come to God for his healing touch and have not found the cure for which they have longed. But the Jesus of the Gospels introduces us to a God who is not one who works according to set rules and formulas, automatically delivering healings to those who know the correct code. But he is one who draws his people into relationship. I suspect that even if that woman in the synagogue had not received the cure for her sickness, she would always have spoken about the God who looked her in the eye and made her stand tall long before her back was straightened. It is this move into a true wellbeing that changes us.

Springtime healing may involve deliverance and cure; but even if it doesn't, an encounter with the tender power of Christ can straighten so much in our lives that has been bent and buckled by the pressures and sorrows of this world.

Reflection

If you were to bump into the lady in our story, what question would you ask her?

Prayer

Healing Christ, you bend down to my level. Let me feel the grasp of your hand, and free all that is stooped in me today.

AWAKENING - BIRTHING FAITH

Then an angel of the Lord said to Philip, 'Get up and go towards the south to the road that goes down from Jerusalem to Gaza'... So he got up and went. Now there was an Ethiopian eunuch... He had come to Jerusalem to worship and was returning home; seated in his chariot, he was reading the prophet Isaiah. Then the Spirit said to Philip, 'Go over to this chariot and join it.' So Philip ran up to it and heard him reading the prophet Isaiah. He asked, 'Do you understand what you are reading?' He replied, 'How can I, unless someone guides me?' And he invited Philip to get in and sit beside him. Now the passage of the scripture that he was reading was this:

'Like a sheep he was led to the slaughter,
    and like a lamb silent before its shearer,
        so he does not open his mouth.
In his humiliation justice was denied him.
    Who can describe his generation?
    For his life is taken away from the earth.'

The eunuch asked Philip, 'About whom, may I ask you, does the prophet say this, about himself or about someone else?' Then Philip began to speak, and starting with this scripture, he proclaimed to him the good news about Jesus. As they were going along the road, they came to some water; and the eunuch said, 'Look, here is water! What is to prevent me from being baptised?'... And Philip baptised him. When they came up out of the water, the Spirit of the Lord snatched Philip away; the eunuch saw him no more, and went on his way rejoicing.

ACTS 8:26–39 (abridged)

In the first century, the road from Jerusalem to Gaza was a busy one. It was one of the routes from Jerusalem to the Mediterranean Sea, so foreigners could often be found travelling upon it. One such returning pilgrim was a dignitary from the far off land of Ethiopia. He served the queen of his country, and as was the somewhat painful custom of the time, it was reckoned that if you were going to have men working closely with a female leader, it was a good deal safer if they were deprived of such equipment as might render them a threat. Although this particular gentleman has lost something of his manhood, he has gained a very senior position in the royal household. Quite whether he thought the exchange was a good deal or not, we don't know. But what we do know was that he was a very thoughtful man with a searching heart. We don't even know what it was that took him to Jerusalem. Something in him felt drawn to that city, and he clearly knew quite a bit about the Jewish faith and was familiar with its language. Maybe the visit to that great city was a lifelong ambition and he had hoped to find some meaning in life there or an encounter with God that would give him what he needed to live out the rest of his days in peace. You get the impression that as he was returning he was not quite satisfied. Perhaps someone has recommended he take a look at the prophet Isaiah, so he makes that his reading material for the long journey home.

As he bumps along in his chariot, he passes his dark finger over the ancient script and, to help himself understand it, he reads it out aloud. He works his way through over 50 chapters of fairly fierce prophecies, including one against Cush,[34] that was getting pretty close to home for him. But once he has worked his way past all the judgements, he then gets to the section of Isaiah which some called 'the Book of Comfort'[35] and it is here that he starts reading about a mysterious figure who is simply called 'the Servant'. Maybe he has read this many times before, or perhaps it is his first time. Either way, he cannot make head nor tail of it. That is, not until someone joins him.

That someone is one of Jesus' apostles. Philip is one of the less prominent disciples, but he comes into his own in chapter 8 of Acts, where we see he has become a very effective preacher. He is also someone who is quite prepared to go wherever God sends him, which on this occasion is the desert road to Gaza. The Ethiopian entourage would have been colourful and impressive, so Philip quickens his pace to catch up with it. He senses he may have some work to do with someone here and, sure enough, as he draws close to the main carriage he hears the foreign voice of an Ethiopian reading out the famous words from Isaiah.

The hospitable Ethiopian is happy for Philip to hitch a lift with him and, in return, he tells Philip he could use some help on a bit of the scripture that is baffling him. So we see this scene in that hot desert place, with sand flying around and the steady beat of horse hoofs and soldiers' feet and the rippling of the canopy protecting this Bible study from the hot sun. The Ethiopian listens intently as this new friend explains that the life so cruelly taken from this earth was a young man who taught the most beautiful things, and worked the most wondrous miracles, and challenged the oppressive rulers and was made to pay for it on a Roman cross. The Ethiopian's eyes are little pools of moisture in this hot desert as he has no trouble imagining this remarkable life that was so cruelly cut short.

But Philip is not finished, for there is more to come. Oh, so much more! And as this maimed African dignitary hears the stories of the empty tomb, the angels, the breakfast on the beach, he starts to get the message that in this world of so much violence, a God has become one of us even to the extent that he suffered terrible mutilation on a cross, only to stun the world into silence as he returned from the grave triumphantly and heralded a whole new era in which death and evil do not have the last word. This Jesus, says Philip, with his eyes shining like the surface of a pool in summer sunshine, is as much alive today as he was then.

How far they proceeded in studying Isaiah we shall never know. What we do know is that at some point the Ethiopian was so taken by the stories of Jesus he did not just want to be a student of the story; he wanted to become part of it. If this Jesus was alive and with them on that desert road, then he wanted to do the simple ritual which was all about washing away the old ways and starting something new. As providence would have it, the desert road took them past one of the several natural springs of water that did a grand job of refreshing weary travellers. The carriage stops and the two men clamber down. It is possible that the Ethiopian removes his clothes at this point and his wounds are there for all to see. But this story he takes with him into the waters, alongside all the other stories that make up his life. Down he goes and feels an old, tired world rinsed away from him and, as he rises up sparkling and laughing, he hears Philip's words of baptism. In delight he splashes the water and, when he drinks from it, it feels like a symbol of the deep waters of life that have flooded his soul. He goes to hug his new-found friend, but Philip is nowhere to be seen. There is a temporary look of sorrow on the Ethiopian's face, but the joy that has entered his heart cannot be quashed. He pulls his robes over his damp body and climbs back into the carriage, and the entourage heads for the coast and the journey home. As far as this Ethiopian is concerned, he is already home.

Christians have used all sorts of expressions to describe this awakening to faith: 'conversion', 'being born again', 'becoming a believer' and 'making a commitment' are among the favourites. None of them really work very well, as it is not an experience that can be neatly defined or categorised. How it happens varies hugely because humans vary hugely, and because God likes to meet each of us in our own way. For some, like the Ethiopian, there is a moment when the penny drops, but for others it can be a long process of gradual awakening. No one can or should prescribe it. And it is not really a once-off experience – there are discoveries about God that happen throughout life.

If we were to visit that Ethiopian chancellor one day in his palace and ask him all about it, it is possible that he may recommend finding a busy desert road and advise us to read a good chunk of Isaiah and wait for a wandering apostle to come along. But I doubt it. From the little we know of him, he seems to have far more sense than to suggest all this is brought about by neat techniques. I suspect he would give us a wide smile and tell us to always travel with the expectation of a divine tap on the shoulder. An awakening to new faith cannot be engineered, but we can always be on the lookout for signs of the risen Jesus who comes to tell us that there is much more to life than we ever imagined.

Reflection

How has faith been awakened in you?

Prayer

Risen Christ, in my journey through this world, will you make your presence felt, and give me the good sense to stop and meet with you, that rivers of living water may flow in and through my life.

SUMMER

The season of
flourishing

INTRODUCTION

For many of us who are fortunate enough to have enjoyed happy childhoods, ask us how we remember the summers of those early days, and we will very likely reply that we recall them as long days of sunshine and warmth; of picnics by riversides and playing in meadows of buttercups; of cooling ourselves with splash pools and ice creams. Warmth and sunlight are the hallmarks of the summer season. But for those who live in northern Europe, we also know that those childhood memories are not the whole truth, because summer can have long stretches of anything but balmy sunshine. And, of course, for those who don't like the heat, if the days do get hot, then summer is a season of struggling to get cool. So, we have to acknowledge that summer can be a mixed blessing.

Shakespeare recognised this in his famous Sonnet 18:

Shall I compare thee to a summer's day?
Thou art more lovely and more temperate:
Rough winds do shake the darling buds of May,
And summer's lease hath all too short a date.

In the poem, Shakespeare recognises that a British summer can be easily spoilt by rough weather and it comes to an end all too soon. But nonetheless he still chooses a summer's day for a comparison with his beloved. His beloved is in fact so radiant and wonderful that her 'eternal summer shall not fade'. For those of us who love the summer season, the bard has registered that longing for the days of warmth and light to never end.

In the Celtic year, the summer season was called *Beltaine* and traditionally began on 1 May, with the summer solstice coming in the middle of the season. Even if the weather is cold and wet at this time of year, nothing can prevent the days lengthening, and no matter how many summers we have passed through in this life, there is always a sense of wonder in our hearts as we arrive in the middle of June and marvel at the ethereal light in the late evening sky.

Regardless of the vagaries of the weather, the season is marked by abundance: the abundance of light and life. Hibernation is a thing of the past, and creation is fully awake and responds to the light and the warmth with the most wonderful flourishing. In the season of the soul, we can also know times when we feel ourselves in a time of flourishing. It might be about celebrating success or special occasions, or a heightened awareness of the gifts we have been given. Summer is a good season for travelling and adventure, and is also the time when many take a holiday, so it can be a season of rest.

It can be all too easy to take summer days for granted and, if we do, we run the risk of missing this season's treasures. The days of flourishing are ones to be acknowledged and cherished. We have to find ways of drawing their life into our roots, so that when the winter days come, they can still serve us with life and energy. Even now, when I am feeling a bit low, I can travel back in the timeline of my life and recall, say, a moment in my childhood when I am lying on my cool bed at the start of the summer holidays. The window is wide open and I hear the swish-swish of the leaf-laden trees as the balmy breeze fills the room with summer blossom fragrance.

This may not be as nostalgic as it sounds. The early peoples of the Bible times learned that there was more to remembering than a yearning for the 'good old days'. The book of Deuteronomy frequently urges the people into disciplines of positive remembrance. Going through times of wintry testing in their wilderness journey to the promised land, they are urged to remember that, though they were once slaves in Egypt, nonetheless God gloriously rescued them through the waters of the Red Sea.[36] Such remembering of summer triumph over wintry oppression empowered them in the tough times. In this regard, Shakespeare was right – summers need not fade. And a wet day in July cannot rinse away from our minds and hearts the experience of the glorious sunshine of the day before.

HOLIDAY - THE FLOURISHING OF REST

Now as [Jesus and his disciples] went on their way, he entered a certain village, where a woman named Martha welcomed him into her home. She had a sister named Mary, who sat at the Lord's feet and listened to what he was saying. But Martha was distracted by her many tasks; so she came to him and asked, 'Lord, do you not care that my sister has left me to do all the work by myself? Tell her then to help me.' But the Lord answered her, 'Martha, Martha, you are worried and distracted by many things; there is need of only one thing. Mary has chosen the better part, which will not be taken away from her.'

LUKE 10:38–42 (see also JOHN 11:1–44; 12:1–7)

There was family of whom Jesus was particularly fond. It was made up of two sisters called Mary and Martha, and their brother Lazarus.[37] Luke records for us a beautifully homely story to do with Jesus visiting them at their house in Bethany as he was on his way to Jerusalem. It must have been tiring travelling over those rough-tracked roads, and Jesus was no doubt delighted to find the home of these friends, where he could put up his feet and enjoy a good meal and a comfortable bed for the night. So on one such day Jesus makes his way to his friends' home.

Martha is first to the door and is both delighted and alarmed to see the figure of Jesus silhouetted in the doorway against the bright late afternoon sun. She hustles him in, apologising for the terrible mess the house is in, and how she was just about to clean it, and if only she had known he was coming she would have got things ready. Jesus stoops through the doorway and enters the cool, dark home, which, to his eyes, looks impeccable. Martha rushes out to the well and frantically pumps cool water into a bucket and then slops it into an earthenware bowl and passes it to her sister. Mary, after greeting him, sits him on the rough wooden chair and removes his sandals, using the water to carefully wash the feet of their welcome guests.

Something troubles Mary as she washes this friend's feet. She remembers a scripture: 'How beautiful upon the mountains are the feet of the messenger who announces peace, who brings good news!'[38] She thinks of the hilly roads traversed by these feet and in her mind she hears the voice of this extraordinary Galilean rabbi telling of a peace that goes to the root of every fear. He has dispersed many fears from Mary's heart. And yet, as she washes his feet, a new fear breaks free from somewhere and causes a frown to darken her face. She suddenly sees these feet as if they have been terribly wounded, for she has a seeing heart. She cannot imagine anyone would want to hurt these feet that have carried good news on the mountains, and yet there is a fear that tells her that these feet are destined to walk through a valley of the shadow of death.

Meanwhile Martha is in the kitchen. She has just rushed round to a neighbour's to borrow some olives and spices. Thankfully, only that morning she had been down to the market and bought a generous supply of fish that was going at a particularly good price. She's now hard at work chopping off the fish heads with dextrous skill. It will make a good stew. It's Mary's day for baking the bread, but there is no sign of it yet. She can be so forgetful, this sister of hers. She calls out to her and reminds her the bread needs baking and the oven's getting cool. The afternoon sun makes the room feel stuffy, and she wipes her forehead with the back of her fishy hand. There is so much to do, and no doubt some of Jesus' friends will come in when they smell the stew, which will add to the numbers. She calls out to her sister again, but there is no reply. Mary is taking so long to come through, so Martha finally bustles through to the front room.

The sight that greets her is enough to light the fuse of the most patient sister. There, with sunlight streaming upon her, is Mary calmly sitting on the floor, gazing up at their guest, with a folded towel beside her. Jesus, with his feet still in the refreshing bowl of water, is saying something to her, and the two are so wrapped in conversation they don't notice the red-faced and fuming woman in the doorway. Martha raises her voice and Mary suddenly feels like she has been startled out of a blessed dream. She sits up guiltily, but Jesus places a hand on her shoulder and she stays where she is.

Martha steps into the room, clutching a knife in one hand and thrusting her hair out of her red face with the other. Her lips are pursed and she turns her gaze from her sister to the visitor who is sitting serenely and apparently quite unaware of the injustice of the situation. So, stepping forward and pointing at her reclining sister, she says, 'Lord, don't you care that this sister of mine is not doing a stroke of work to help me. Tell her to get up off her lazy backside and come and pull her weight!'

Mary turns and looks anxiously at Jesus. She really wants to get up now and appease her sister, but Jesus' hand remains firmly on her shoulder. He looks at Martha and says, 'Come here, Martha – come and sit for a moment here.' He points to the goatskin mat on the floor. Mary moves to make space for her sister. Martha looks back anxiously at the uncooked food on the table behind her. She wants to protest, but when she looks back at her visitor, she knows she must listen to him. It's just something about him. He looks so understandingly at her. He knows her so very well. She places the knife on a table, and then reluctantly moves to the mat and kneels awkwardly on it, keeping some distance from her idle sister.

Jesus smiles a tender smile as he says, 'Martha, so much in life worries and distracts you.' He says more things that she does not fully hear, for she feels like one who has been found out. Yes, it is true, all her life she has been riddled by anxiety – so much has had to be done, got ready, put straight, sorted out, cleaned, cooked, mended and swept. She looks at her sister and sees in her something for which she has yearned all her life: serenity. She always thought it was at best a gift, and at worst; laziness. But now as she looks at her gentle sister kneeling by this dear friend, she realises it has been simply her choice. She has chosen to welcome stillness and rest into her life, and when she does, the world has not fallen apart without her.

Martha wipes her hand on her apron thoughtfully and looks down at her hands that are always restless and busy. Suddenly, her frantic busyness looks quite absurd. In her mind she sees herself bustling around in the kitchen, crashing around with pots and pans. As she does so, she feels something in her chest – an unfamiliar emotion that is pushing its way to the surface. Try as she might, she fails to suppress it. Her face finally gives way and for a moment Mary and Jesus are unsure if she is about to sneeze, sob or laugh. They do not have to wait long to find out, for the conscientious and hard-working Martha is suddenly beside herself with laughter.

Mary is astonished – she has never seen this! The sight is so funny and unexpected that she starts to chuckle, then giggles and finally lets out a shriek of laughter. And above the sound of their whoops and hollerings is a roar of delight from the seated rabbi who stamps his feet in the bowl, spraying the sisters with water, which simply adds to their helpless howls.

The 'Protestant work ethic', as it is sometimes called, has been the bugbear of many Christian people. They have naïvely supposed that God is impressed by relentless industriousness and high activity. But the story of Martha and Mary challenges this. Of course, at some point in that story, someone would need to get up and make a meal – maybe it was Jesus? But what seems to shine clear in this story is that there are times in life when God wants us to simply sit down and have a good rest and stop our rushing around. If we will spend just a few moments in the presence of God, in whatever way works for us, we may well be surprised by what we discover. We may find ways of living more restfully and peacefully in this world.

We should not judge Martha just by this tale. In the story of the raising of her brother back to life, it is Martha who, after a characteristic reprimand to Jesus for his lateness, then looks him in the eye and says without a shadow of hesitation or doubt, 'Lord, I believe that you are the Messiah, the Son of God.'[39] It is most likely that she discerned this because she had learned to draw her mind away from the busy preoccupations of life, to give space for deeper thinking and reflecting. We all need seasons of stillness to release ourselves from the demands of everyday life. It is by no means uncommon that such seasons become times when faith is given space to rise to the surface and we discover new things about God and ourselves.

Reflection

How is the work/rest rhythm of your life? Does it need reviewing?

Prayer

When I become too busy and driven, Lord, lead me to better rhythms and a gentler pace.

BIRTHDAY – THE FLOURISHING OF YOU

For everything there is a season, and a time for every matter under heaven:
    a time to be born, and a time to die;
    a time to plant, and a time to pluck up what is planted;
    a time to kill, and a time to heal;
    a time to break down, and a time to build up;
    a time to weep, and a time to laugh;
    a time to mourn, and a time to dance;
    a time to throw away stones, and a time to gather stones together;
    a time to embrace, and a time to refrain from embracing;
    a time to seek, and a time to lose;
    a time to keep, and a time to throw away;
    a time to tear, and a time to sew;
    a time to keep silence, and a time to speak;
    a time to love, and a time to hate;
    a time for war, and a time for peace.

ECCLESIASTES 3:1–8 (see also all of ECCLESIASTES)

There is no date in the calendar quite like your birthday. Although millions of other humans share this date as their birthday, you know it is peculiarly yours. If you were fortunate to have had a happy childhood, then your birthday probably had a special magic about it. From the moment you woke up, you were treated as a dignitary and your day was full of gifts and special treats. This day was set aside to celebrate *you*. Even when you grew up, the day did not completely lose its magic. As time went on and you became an adult, you started to worry about the accumulation of years, and birthdays started to carry a mixed message: yes, you might be special for a day, but look how many years are now piling up behind you – and look at the signs of age creeping upon your body. Nonetheless, despite our sighs about the effects of ageing, every birthday is an opportunity to reflect on the uniqueness of you, and to consider this miraculous gift of life that is yours.

To help you reflect in this way, you could do no better than dip into the book of Ecclesiastes. Granted, it is one of the most puzzling books of the Bible, and at first sight it seems to be written by an ageing cynic who has been round the block once too often. But a closer study of this intriguing book reveals a very honest exploration of life – of what matters and what doesn't, and what is genuine and what is false. The writer is willing to look at some of the tough questions he has had to face during his life to do with suffering and injustice, and he is not prepared to settle for easy off-the-peg official answers. He is willing to live in the questions, rather than hasten to superficial answers.

No one knows quite who was the author of this book. It might have been the great and wise King Solomon, but most seem to think it was a rather more humble person writing some years later. He calls himself *Qoheleth*, a Hebrew word that has been variously translated 'preacher', 'philosopher' and 'teacher' and in many respects he is all of these. Whoever he was, he was someone writing towards the end of his life and he feels it is time to share what he has learned during his long years on this planet.

So whether you are young in years or older, it might be an idea to go and visit this old man and see what he has to say to you on this day when you are celebrating the fact that once upon a time on this calendar day, you emerged from your mother's womb to take your place in this world. Come and take a good look at this philosopher. Maybe you find him sitting at a rough wooden table in the market place, clasping a cup of beer. The marks of the froth glisten on his stringy grey beard. There is not much hair covering his sun-tanned dome. The mottled, thin skin of his forehead descends to some whiskery eyebrows that arch over restless and searching eyes that seem to be darting here and there in keen anticipation. They cannot see you too clearly, but they know you are there as you settle at the table with him. You sit with him and, whether you like it or not, you have to listen to all that he wants to tell you on this, your royal day.

And so he tells you that he has learned something very significant about time: he says there is a rhythm in life, a turning of the seasons so that when things come and go, they do so in a harmony, in a pattern. The secret is to do your best to fall into this pattern, to recognise that one day it will be right to plant the seed, but on another day you must pluck the fruit. There will be times in life when it is time to end something such as a job or a relationship or an old grudge, whereas on another day it will be all about taking what is fragile and wounded and bringing it back to life. Round and round he goes with all kinds of life situations, so that you are almost dizzy by the end of it. But he goes on and tells you in his husky voice, 'He has made everything suitable for its time. And what's more, he has put a sense of past and future into your mind. So, for goodness' sake, make the most of this one precious life you have been given, and enjoy the good things that come your way.'[40]

As he sips his beer, he looks at you and makes you uncomfortable, because this kind of looking is a searching of your inner world and none of us enjoy being scrutinised too much. But there is something kind in those penetrating eyes. 'Remember your creator,' he says, not waiting to find out whether you are a believer or not. He has seen lots of suffering and brutality and has asked his fair share of painful and puzzling questions. But when it comes down to it, all that puzzlement and pain has not robbed him from a conviction that there is a creator behind it all, and the only way to make sense of it is to somehow find some connection with the one who created you.

Just as you are drawing breath to offer a counterargument, he leans forward and grasps you with his bony and brittle hand and says almost in a whisper, 'The time will come when your eyes will grow misty as mine have done: the sun and the light and the moon and the stars are darkened. And then, my friend, one day the silver cord of this life will be snapped and the golden bowl will be smashed – the pitcher broken at the fountain, and the wheel shattered at the cistern.' With his other hand he sweeps some sand from the table, 'And the dust returns to the earth as it was, and the breath returns to the God who gave it. Vanity of vanities, my friend!'[41] His laugh reveals a mouth that has lost most of its teeth. He takes a sip of beer and nods at you.

As you sip your own beer, you wonder if he is telling you good news or bad. Is he saying make the most of life, or is he saying it's all a chasing after a wind that you can never hope to catch? And if you do get round to asking him about that, then it's likely he will tell you that the choice is yours. For what this old sage is saying in the words of his ancient book is that life is a most precious and finite gift, and it is our choice to use our life and its seasons fully and fruitfully. We cannot control what happens to us in life, but we can make choices about how we respond.

On your birthday especially, it is wise to creep away from the party for a few moments, and step outside briefly to have a word with that old man in the marketplace. He loves celebrations and he will be pleased to hear about your birthday. But he will probably also remind you that your wonderful, unique life, as well as the beautiful world in which you have the good fortune to dwell, have been fashioned by a divine creator who, from the moment you became life in your mother's womb, has had purposes for you. This creator is one who is well aware that you have been placed in a world in which there are precious few straight answers. But Qoheleth has confidence that each of us has the capacity to hold mystery – we can see that in this world there is so much vanity, waste and unfairness. But we don't have to settle down with a shrug of the shoulders bemoaning our lot and filing complaints. The old man leans back in his chair, dips his head and looks hard at you. 'The wise have eyes in their heads,' he says with a wry smile, and, leaning forward, adds, 'but fools walk in the darkness.'[42] He knows that wisdom does not protect you from hard or tough situations, but the point is you can have eyes that can see. Get used to this kind of seeing, this precious gift of wisdom, and you soon find that wisdom actually makes your face shine and those hard frowns are softened.[43]

So, if you are reading this on your birthday, how about asking your creator for a very special present – the gift of wisdom, the gift of eyes? Don't judge yourself by the foolish fashion magazines and bland statements of celebrities. Don't be cowed by the harsh shouts of your accusers, nor by your failures. Take a step closer to your creator, who sees you quite differently to all of that. Listen for his benediction. Become yourself. In fact, this is not a gift just for birthdays – every day of the year should have a birthday moment in it: a moment when you celebrate again the person God has made you to be. Take a sip of Qoheleth's medicine – a true wisdom fermented in the knowledge that you are the beloved of your creator.

Reflection

What does wisdom mean to you?

Prayer

For it was you who formed my inward parts; you knit me together in my mother's womb. I praise you, for I am fearfully and wonderfully made. Wonderful are your works; that I know very well.[44]

ROUSING – THE FLOURISHING OF JUSTICE

In those days John the Baptist appeared in the wilderness of Judea, proclaiming, 'Repent, for the kingdom of heaven has come near.' This is the one of whom the prophet Isaiah spoke when he said,
> 'The voice of one crying out in the wilderness:
> "Prepare the way of the Lord,
>   make his paths straight."'

Now John wore clothing of camel's hair with a leather belt around his waist, and his food was locusts and wild honey. Then the people of Jerusalem and all Judea were going out to him, and all the region along the Jordan, and they were baptised by him in the river Jordan, confessing their sins.

But when he saw many Pharisees and Sadducees coming for baptism, he said to them, 'You brood of vipers! Who warned you to flee from the wrath to come? Bear fruit worthy of repentance. Do not presume to say to yourselves, "We have Abraham as our ancestor"; for I tell you, God is able from these stones to raise up children to Abraham. Even now the axe is lying at the root of the trees; every tree therefore that does not bear good fruit is cut down and thrown into the fire.

MATTHEW 3:1–10 (see also MATTHEW 3:11–17; 14:1–13)

Street preachers are a phenomenon that has been around for years. What is a little more unusual is a desert preacher. It's one thing to plant your lectern in the precincts of Exeter Cathedral on a Saturday afternoon, but quite another to set up shop in a remote part of Dartmoor. The chances are that the congregation there would not amount to much more than a high-flying lark and a puzzled hare.

However, centuries ago one such preacher did the unthinkable and made his way to a stream that flowed through the Judean Desert, and there let rip with such a stormy gospel message that thousands dropped their shopping bags and hightailed it into the wilderness to catch sight of this phenomenon. The preacher did look a bit weird as he wore a simple robe of camel hair, and if you took a closer look you'd see his hands were covered in bee stings as he favoured honey-covered locusts for his main meal of the day.

No doubt there was no shortage of those who took one look at the apparent religious maniac, had a laugh, and made their way home. However, huge numbers, far from finding him off-putting, hung around because they felt he had something really important to say. Yes, they did indeed hear the words 'sin' and 'repent', but they were in the context of a message that was full of life and hope, and many of those who heard this message decided to make that message stick in their hearts by engaging in the relatively new ritual of baptism.

The Gospel writers summon up the scene so clearly. John is standing there, knee-deep at the edge of the river. A line of men, women and children are snaking their way from the dusty roadside into the water to meet this baptiser. John speaks private words to each one, and then lowers them into the flowing stream. Up each one comes, their faces gleaming in the bright sunshine. Some look dazed, some delighted and some in tears. Back they go to the riverbank, and a few stay there warming themselves in the sun and looking to the skies with gratitude. All these people look much the same: there is nothing particularly that distinguishes any of the people; they are all fairly poor, and can't afford elegant clothes.

However, along come a couple of men who do look different. They are careful not to touch anyone in the crowd of people lest they should make contact with something that would defile them. Their dress marks them out from the others – the distinctive black and white striped shawl and heavy dark robe. They don't follow the crowd into the river, but stay by the roadside. It is time for their prayers, so they bend as low as they can and commence their devotions. Those around them look awkward, made to feel guilty again, for they know they are not as prayerful as these religious professionals. These apparent experts are the Pharisees. They are the ones who know exactly how religion should be done, and a self-proclaimed prophet dousing people in the river Jordan is definitely not the correct way. When they finish their prayers they stand together, both with arms folded and their bearded faces creased in disapproval. They are accustomed to receiving the greatest respect, so it somewhat catches them off their guard when they hear the voice of the baptiser in the river suddenly rise to a roar. They look up and see he has paused from his heretical baptising ritual and is addressing his remarks directly at them.

The preacher points his dripping and trembling arm at them and starts to shout things that stun the crowd into silence. He has been so gentle with them, and yet to these Pharisees he is a fuming fury. He roars at the two smart professionals on the bank and calls them a 'brood of vipers', and warns that all their posh, religiously correct ways are nothing more than fruitless trees that should be hacked down and chucked on the fire. He is saying all this to the religious VIPs to whom no one so much as ever dared utter a word of complaint for fear of stirring the wrath of God. And yet, the people feel a thrill of truth as they hear John's words. Perhaps they have all always known, but have been too afraid to admit, that the Pharisees are power-hungry instead of humble, keeping people away from God instead of drawing them to a better knowledge of him. Perhaps it is the Pharisees who are responsible for their view of God as an austere and frightening deity, who can be offended by the slightest misconduct. And perhaps, only perhaps, the Pharisees know and embrace this, for there's nothing like religious fear to keep people in their places.

When John eventually finishes his tirade, he turns back to a couple standing near him and smiles kindly before plunging them into the stream. The Pharisees are dumbfounded and, completely lost for words in their intense indignation, they about turn and stomp their way back to Jerusalem.

In many ways, John's story feels familiar, because similar themes have been repeated time and time again in history. In communities of deep oppression, someone rises above that oppression and finds words and actions that eventually free the people. In the mid 1950s, on a cold December morning in Montgomery, Alabama, Rosa Parks climbed aboard her bus on her way to work as a seamstress. As was the dreadful custom of the time, she had to sit in the 'coloured' section of the bus. The 'white' section of the bus soon filled up, and the rules stated that when the white section was full, those in the coloured section had to surrender their seats to white people, on the assumption that white skin had more right to be seated than black. When Rosa was told to move to allow a white man to sit in her place, she promptly placed her bag on her knee and refused to budge, much to the shock and disgust of the white section of the bus. It was a spark of protest that had been ignited by her horror of the injustice of segregation. Inspired by her example, the leaders of her community organised a bus boycott. One of those leaders was a young man called Revd Dr Martin Luther King. The rest, as they say, is history.

The transformation of our society for the better is formed by people who at some point in their lives move from passive observance to passionate action. There is a moment when something snaps and that which was once only dreamed of becomes reality. A winter of discontent becomes a summer of vibrant action. Thus a young man makes his way to a river and changes people's view of God. A young woman refuses to budge from her seat on the bus, and in time changes people's view of people.

There are moments in all our lives when we sense something is about to give way. A passion, a longing, a dream starts to shout so loudly within us, we cannot bear to go on living as we are, and we have to do something. It might be something highly risky, as it was with John and Rosa. But often it is not as dramatic as that – it can be a disturbance that leads to such decisions as joining a political party or becoming actively involved in a cause, or volunteering services to a charity that is changing people's lives. These seasons of rousing can be thrilling, but seldom are they without cost. John the Baptist's time was cut short by imprisonment and martyrdom. But I think if we were to make our way down to the damp cell where he was incarcerated by the cruel Herod, he would look us hard in the eye and say, 'But I have seen him – I have seen the beloved of God. I have seen the one who will lead us all home.' I suppose he might even have said, 'I have a dream that one day every valley shall be exalted, and every hill and mountain be laid low, the rough places will be made plain, and the crooked places will be made straight; "and the glory of the Lord shall be revealed and all flesh shall see it together".'[45]

In the summertime of the soul, there can be these surgings of the Spirit – prophetic responses to injustices in our world. They can feel both exciting and troublesome, but either way they need listening to. Such rousings can change the world.

Reflection

Albert Einstein once wrote, 'The world will not be destroyed by those who do evil, but by those who watch them without doing anything.'[46]

Prayer

O Lord, give me ears to hear and courage to act.

RELEASE – THE
FLOURISHING OF FREEDOM

> One day, as we [Paul and others] were going to the place
> of prayer, we met a slave-girl who had a spirit of divination
> and brought her owners a great deal of money by fortune-
> telling. While she followed Paul and us, she would cry out,
> 'These men are slaves of the Most High God, who proclaim
> to you a way of salvation.' She kept doing this for many days.
> But Paul, very much annoyed, turned and said to the spirit,
> 'I order you in the name of Jesus Christ to come out of her.'
> And it came out that very hour.
>
> ACTS 16:16–18 (see also ACTS 16:19–40)

The summer season carries with it a sense of freedom. It is a season
which, if it is behaving itself properly, is one in which you can throw
open the windows, leave doors ajar without risking draughts, kick
off your shoes and saunter outside without having to shield yourself
against the cold. Furthermore, when it comes to the holiday season,
children find themselves free of the normal school routines and
pressures, and many people take their holidays and are free of the
office, the emails, the phone calls and all the pressing demands of their
work. The freedom of a holiday can feel like venturing into an open
world with plenty of space for rest and for exploration. Conversely, for
some, the ending of the holidays can feel like a return to a far more
confined world of pressures, deadlines, demands and responsibilities.

The theme of freedom is never far from the pages of the Bible and
this story from Acts is one such example. We journey back to first-
century Asia Minor, and we are in the company of Paul and Silas, two
men who were on an extraordinary adventure telling the Roman

world about the good news of the God who had come to earth in the form of Jesus – the God who had become one of us so that we could find our freedom. They eventually cross over the Aegean Sea to the city of Philippi, and it is there they stumble across a girl whose life has been entangled by slavery and darkness.

We know very little about this girl. In fact, if you read chapter 16 of Acts too fast you could easily miss her, and she would have probably been missed from the records altogether if she had not inadvertently been the cause of a near riot in the city, a flogging and jailing of Paul and Silas, and their subsequent miraculous release. But today I want to spend time with her story and get to know her a little without speeding on to the stories of floggings, prisons and earthquakes. And so I bring her in from the edge of the page and try and get a closer look at her.

I know nothing about the life of slaves in Philippi in the first century, so I will just have to use my imagination and do some guesswork. As I do so, I see the slave girl there at the side of one of the busy, bustling streets. Though the climate is warm, I nonetheless see her wrapped up in a brown cloak and looking cold. There are dark lines under her eyes, and if I'm not mistaken they have been painted on to give her a more mysterious, occult appearance. She is sitting on a stool that is perched on the cobbled pavement and her back is to a rough brick wall. The street is wet from recent rainfall and the air is stale with the sour odour of damp stones and horse dung. She is leaning forward with her chin resting on her upturned right hand, and she gazes forward as if she is looking to a far horizon.

Next to her stand a couple of men who appear to have some connection with the girl, for I see one of them grasp hold of a passing stranger and talk to them about the girl. He keeps pulling at the girl's shoulder as he aims to do business with this passerby. The girl is unmoved by this, and keeps gazing out to whatever it is she is gazing out at. The stranger clearly is not interested in the girl, and he hurries on up the street. These then are the girl's two owners and it is her current lot in life to earn money for them through her fortune telling.

One of the men's deep voices rises high above the hubbub of the street, 'Come and get your fortune told by this beautiful little witch. She will tell you all you need to know. Come on, come on, I'm asking a fair price.' Again, the girl makes no movement. But it is at this moment I spot Paul and his friends turning into this street. The owners see an opportunity for trade. The visitors notice the girl straightaway and are about to speak to her, when she shivers and abruptly comes to life. She looks aghast and springs up from her stool, knocking it over with a clatter causing others in the street to turn round and look. She looks intently at the visitors, as if she recognises them or at least something in them, and, bending forward, she stretches out her thin arm and points hard at them. With a voice far louder than I thought her little frame could manage, she yells, 'These men are slaves of the Most High God...' and she repeats it again and again, screaming to the world that they are carrying a message of salvation, though something about the way she shrieks this out makes it sound like anything but a message of good news.

The owners look anxious – they know something is not right. Paul and his friend Silas walk calmly towards the swaying girl whose cries dry up as they approach her. She halts her swaying and looks at them. She clearly sees something in these men that she has not seen before. She says nothing, but the expression on her face is a clear cry for help. Paul and Silas look on her with great compassion, but then surprisingly Paul's look changes and fierce anger blazes from his eyes. He raises his voice and cries out a command that clearly makes no sense to her, but does to something within her. His voice echoes off the nearby buildings before a hush settles on the street. Silas reaches towards her, for she staggers for a moment like a drunkard. He catches her and lowers her gently to the street where she kneels and rubs her eyes several times before opening them wide. These eyes are different. The tears cause them to sparkle as she grips the arms of Silas. She smiles – an open smile that quickly turns into laughter, the laughter of the free.

Her two owners immediately see that something has gone very badly wrong. This lucrative source of income looks like it might suddenly have dried up and the scandalous cause of this disaster are these two foreigners. And so the story continues with Paul and Silas being imprisoned, and yet so free inwardly that they sing their way out of jail within hours of arriving. The message of freedom within them is one that cannot be bound by occult powers, human malevolence or prison bars. We don't know what became of the slave girl after this story, but I like to think she was taken in by local friends of Paul and Silas and, who knows, perhaps she herself became a minister of the gospel, bringing freedom and release to others.

There are sadly many people in this world who have encountered the forces of darkness that have held their souls prisoner, and there are also many people held in different kinds of slavery, suffering because of the selfishness and greed of others. But this little story in the heart of Acts reminds me that the Jesus who walked this earth and offered release to so many also lived in the likes of Paul, Silas and countless Christians after him, and he lives even in the likes of me. It is he who has the word to bring freedom to my soul. And it is he who may catch my attention at any moment, calling me to bring his freedom to others.

Reflection

What does this story of the slave girl say to you? What needs releasing in your soul? How can you be used today to bring freedom to others?

Prayer

Liberator Jesus, visit my soul and set me free. And give me the courage to bring your freedom to others.

ABUNDANCE – THE FLOURISHING OF WEALTH

When the queen of Sheba heard of the fame of Solomon (fame due to the name of the Lord), she came to test him with hard questions. She came to Jerusalem with a very great retinue, with camels bearing spices, and very much gold, and precious stones; and when she came to Solomon, she told him all that was on her mind. Solomon answered all her questions; there was nothing hidden from the king that he could not explain to her. When the queen of Sheba had observed all the wisdom of Solomon, the house that he had built, the food of his table, the seating of his officials, and the attendance of his servants, their clothing, his valets, and his burnt-offerings that he offered at the house of the Lord, there was no more spirit in her.

1 KINGS 10:1–5 (see also 1 KINGS 10:6—11:13; MATTHEW 6:25–34)

Browsing through a daily newspaper not so long ago, I spotted a picture of a very happy-looking couple called David and Carol who between them were holding a giant cheque for the phenomenal amount of £33,035,323. They were the triumphant winners of the lottery and, not surprisingly, they looked very pleased about it, if somewhat astonished. I paused and, like most others glancing at that page, I started to wonder what it would be like to come into such a vast sum of money. Imaginations of a life of extravagance started to fill my mind.

There is someone in the Bible who also amassed unimaginable wealth, and that person was Solomon, the son of King David and Bathsheba. Solomon was the king of Israel and, though his kingdom was relatively small, his prosperity was fabulous, so fabulous that the queen of a far-off land decided to come and see for herself this man and his wealth. What she had heard was that this king of Israel was not only greatly blessed with material wealth, but he was also well supplied with wisdom, and it seems that it was this treasure she was particularly after. However, knowing he had an eye for luxury items, she brought a fair few with her on her journey from Sheba (now modern-day Yemen).

And so we can imagine this Arabian queen making her way up the winding road to Jerusalem with a cortege of personnel guiding a large number of grunting gold- and spice-laden camels. She makes her way to the recently built and luxurious palace and there she is introduced to the great King Solomon. She is ushered into a great hall and they both settle in throne-like chairs as exotic fruits and fine wines are placed before them. An interpreter sits on a stool between them. A slave wafts a broad palm branch to cool the royal conclave.

How would it be if you were one of the many servants standing in that warm and grand hall that day? You would see the queen leaning forward and plucking a lush grape from the gold bowl in front of her and eagerly questioning the Israelite king. You can't quite hear what they are saying, but you can see that every time she asks a question, the king confidently answers her, clearly to her satisfaction. She nods with admiration and delight. The morning becomes afternoon, and servants bring food and refreshment, but the earnest conversation never abates. The queen of Sheba's eyes gleam in delight at the wisdom she is hearing from the erudite lips of this king.

When it is clear that she has exhausted all her questions, she gives a signal to one of her attendants who claps his hands to someone standing near the door. The king looks with interest, and then his wise face lights up as dark-skinned and broad-shouldered men bring in trays of heavy and shiny gold and baskets full of twinkling precious gems. Following them, some women enter carrying beautifully wrapped parcels that fill the room with the most exquisite fragrances of Arabian spices. You look on in astonishment at this exotic feast of abundance, but none are more delighted than King Solomon, who grasps the hand of the dignified queen and thanks her profusely. He has gained more riches and she has gained more wisdom – and a few pricey souvenirs from the king for good measure.

As a servant, you look on with a mix of feelings. You stand so close to this king and queen and yet their wealth is far removed from your life experience. You perhaps imagine what it would be like if one of those trays of gold had been passed to you – what freedoms and wonders would come your way with such wealth. You inhale the scent of the delicious cinnamon and cardamom and imagine a world in which such scents and flavours were part of everyday life. But soon you will return to your humble home, hoping there will be enough food on the table for your family tonight.

Since ancient times, the world has known great inequalities of wealth. And in our own experience, we may well have known seasons where things have been very tight, and other times when there has been an abundance of money and possessions. In times of abundance, it might be worth remembering Solomon and his fabulous wealth. Whether all that wealth made him happy is hard to say. He almost certainly would have subscribed to the theology of the time that such wealth was a sign of God's blessing. But, if you read on in his story, things take a turn for the worse for Solomon. He becomes somewhat blasé in his wealth and risks breaking a few of the rules of the God who has blessed him. One of his worst offences was to marry foreign wives, who bring with them their own religions – something God told him would bring trouble, and trouble it does bring for him and his kingdom. All that wealth did not bring security – not by any means.

Centuries later, another wise man walked the same land. He was a good deal poorer than Solomon, but even wiser. He mustered a group of disciples around him and taught them many things about money and possessions. In one of his famous bits of teaching, he referred to Solomon. He noticed that his friends worried a good deal about money and possessions, so he said:

> Therefore I tell you, do not worry about your life, what you will eat or what you will drink, or about your body, what you will wear. Is not life more than food, and the body more than clothing? Look at the birds of the air; they neither sow nor reap nor gather into barns, and yet your heavenly Father feeds them. Are you not of more value than they? And can any of you by worrying add a single hour to your span of life? And why do you worry about clothing? Consider the lilies of the field, how they grow; they neither toil nor spin, yet I tell you, even Solomon in all his glory was not clothed like one of these… Strive first for the kingdom of God and his righteousness, and all these things will be given to you as well.[47]

I am sure that at least one of those disciples took the trouble to find a lily in the field soon after that conversation and studied it hard. They thought of the great King Solomon in his sumptuous, fine robes sitting in his royal chamber enjoying unimaginable prosperity; then they cradled the lily in their hand and started to see it in a new light. In this light, it became the most valuable of possessions that money could not buy. They began to get it. Jesus' words have the habit of bringing us to our true senses and discovering what is really valuable.

Wealth is a good servant but a poor master. No doubt those winners of the lottery have to learn this. But what I notice, reading the reports of those who have been winners, is that they often testify to the same thing, expressed well by one of the winners, who said, 'But the most rewarding part of my win has been that I am able to help out my family and support charities close to my heart.'[48] Perhaps the real wisdom that is required for any season of wealth is the wisdom that responds to prosperity with gratitude and generosity. Jesus tells us that, whether we are rich or poor, the key to peace of mind is seeking the kingdom of God. If we are not sure what that is, then we need to embark on a quest for wisdom – maybe there is an equivalent of the queen of Sheba not too far away who will be happy to tell us her story.

Reflection

If you are in a season of prosperity, take time to reflect on how this is influencing your values. If it is a season of scarcity, what do Jesus' words quoted in this passage say to you today?

Prayer

Creator God, help me to live the truth of these words of the apostle Paul: 'I know what it is to have little, and I know what it is to have plenty. In any and all circumstances I have learned the secret of being well-fed and of going hungry, of having plenty and of being in need.'[49]

SALVATION – THE FLOURISHING OF GRATITUDE

He entered Jericho and was passing through it. A man was there named Zacchaeus; he was a chief tax-collector and was rich. He was trying to see who Jesus was, but on account of the crowd he could not, because he was short in stature. So he ran ahead and climbed a sycamore tree to see him, because he was going to pass that way. When Jesus came to the place, he looked up and said to him, 'Zacchaeus, hurry and come down; for I must stay at your house today.' So he hurried down and was happy to welcome him. All who saw it began to grumble and said, 'He has gone to be the guest of one who is a sinner.' Zacchaeus stood there and said to the Lord, 'Look, half of my possessions, Lord, I will give to the poor; and if I have defrauded anyone of anything, I will pay back four times as much.' Then Jesus said to him, 'Today salvation has come to this house, because he too is a son of Abraham. For the Son of Man came to seek out and to save the lost.'

LUKE 19:1–10

'Are you saved?' This is a fairly blunt question sometimes asked by pop-up street evangelists who imagine that the concept of salvation is one that preoccupies your mind on a daily basis, and if it doesn't it should. A long time ago, when I was a keen young Christian, I tried it myself in a shopping precinct and discovered that such a question was greeted with a range of responses, ranging from kindly bafflement to hostile reproach. If I remember rightly, the experiment lasted no longer than 45 minutes and left me with a fairly strong sense of guilt and failure, causing me to retreat to a nearby coffee shop for a speedy return to normality. And yet, while I would never use this kind of insensitive approach again, I find myself nonetheless intrigued by the concept. We are all fascinated by genuine stories of rescue and salvation – hostages being saved from a horrifying death by skilful negotiators and rescue teams; swimmers caught in a dangerous current being saved by a courageous lifeboat crew; paramedics saving a child's life after a road traffic accident; mountain rescue teams saving the lives of walkers who took a wrong turn as the weather broke. When we hear of such stories of people being saved, we are thrilled.

In the story of Zacchaeus, Jesus uses these terms 'salvation' and 'saved', but the story does not start with him randomly grabbing Zacchaeus' attention on a street corner nor plucking him from a raging sea. It starts with a glance into the leafy branches of a sycamore tree.

Our storyteller, Luke, tells us that Zacchaeus' profession was tax collection. There are doubtless very few popular tax collectors in history, but in Jesus' day they were a particularly despised species, because most were unscrupulous and made a great deal of money from exploiting the poor. It seems that the wealthy Zacchaeus was no exception. So there he is, just about to settle down for a siesta in a shady precinct of his big villa on the outskirts of Jericho, when he hears a commotion coming down the road. His initial irritation at being disturbed from his rest changes to interest when he hears someone shouting that Jesus is coming into the town. He has heard interesting things about this subversive rabbi and his curiosity gets the better of him. He nips out of his villa, and finds a tree that lines the route. If he stood in the crowd he would stand little chance of seeing anything – besides, he is so unpopular with the people they would certainly shove him to the back. So he hauls himself up on to a leafy branch that arches across the sandy track.

He is safely hidden as the crowd approaches. He leans forward to get a clearer view. What is it about this rabbi that is getting the people so excited? He looks like any other rabbi as far as he can see. And yet something is different – he seems to be somehow *close* to the people – less aloof. He is laughing with them and even greets one of them with a bear hug. There is a human holiness in this man, quite different from the trumped up holiness of the religious people he knows.

As the noisy crowd draws nearer, Zacchaeus becomes aware of a deep sense of shame as he thinks about his lifestyle and his ill-gotten gains, and he pulls himself back trying to hide himself in his leafy den. But it is just at this point that the crowd stops its slow progress. Why have they stopped? He hardly dares look. He freezes and hopes against hope that he can remain hidden by the leaves. But then he hears it – his name. This curious rabbi is standing directly below him and is calling his name. There is something about the tone of voice that arouses not his fears, but his hopes. It is that hope that gives Zacchaeus the confidence to lean forward from his branch and peer down at the upturned face of the travelling rabbi. Jesus looks at Zacchaeus with the expression of one greeting a long-lost friend.

What comes next is the last thing Zacchaeus expects to hear. Jesus is asking to stay at his house. Everyone knows that respectable religious people, especially rabbis, do not go into a sinner's home. If Jesus so much as takes one step into the grounds of his home, he will be tainted and it will take an elaborate ritual to cleanse him from his dirtiness. For a few moments Zacchaeus stares at this unorthodox rabbi in disbelief, but it is not long before a smile of delight replaces his frown of uncertainty.

He scrambles down from his tree and stands before the rabbi. He brushes twigs and leaves from his robes and looks up at the one who has called him. To the shock and astonishment of the onlookers, Jesus makes to go into his house. Zacchaeus abruptly stops him at the gate. Something extraordinary is churning inside the heart of this once tight-fisted tax gatherer. There are voices in the crowd now barking complaints not just at Zacchaeus but at Jesus as well. Zacchaeus looks nervously at the angry faces – faces he knows only too well. He is all too familiar with their hatred. He used to return hatred with hatred, but now something has been turned upside down in his soul and he has little idea why. All he knows is that a holy man has looked upon him with a look he never imagined he could receive. It is a look that has exposed the hollow chambers of his selfish heart. But it also causes it to start to see things it has never seen before.

His heart sees the faces of the angry onlookers and for the first time perceives why they are angry. He sees the hurt behind the eyes, and feels in his changing heart the injustice of his former ways. He looks beseechingly at the rabbi who is standing at the gate of his home, and then hears his own voice spoken in a tone he hardly recognises: 'Lord,' he says, sweeping his arm over his estate, 'I shall give half of all of this away and, where I have fleeced these people, then I will gladly repay them with interest.' This stuns the crowd into silence and it is at this point that Jesus proclaims to the crowd, 'Today, salvation has come to this house.'

If after this encounter with Jesus you happened to bump into Zacchaeus in the street and asked him, 'Are you saved?', you can be fairly certain that his eyes would well up and he would look up at you with the tenderness of a reformed soul and say, 'Oh yes! Oh, most definitely yes!' And the winsome smile would tell you that this was genuine salvation. Something in his humanity was in grave peril, and he was rescued.

Genuine salvation begins with revelation. It is a moment of seeing what we are made of and we are likely to discover a tangled mix of good and ill. The saving part is the discovery that the eyes of God look upon it all with a gaze of love. The fruit of this kind of salvation is not a life of groveling penance, nor the flaunting of a superior saintliness. It will be a lifestyle of gratitude that spills over into carefree generosity to those around us. Any of us, at any time, can find ourselves disturbed in our normal routines of life when we discover that Jesus is attracting our attention and calls us into a new healed way of life. If we will do our equivalent of vulnerably climbing down from our lofty trees, we will discover we are met by the God who beckons us into summertime salvation.

Reflection

Are you saved?

Prayer

Visit the home of my heart this day, dear Lord, and release streams of salvation in and through me.

CELEBRATION – THE FLOURISHING OF COMMUNITY

On the third day there was a wedding in Cana of Galilee, and the mother of Jesus was there. Jesus and his disciples had also been invited to the wedding. When the wine gave out, the mother of Jesus said to him, 'They have no wine.' And Jesus said to her, 'Woman, what concern is that to you and to me? My hour has not yet come.' His mother said to the servants, 'Do whatever he tells you.' Now standing there were six stone water-jars for the Jewish rites of purification, each holding twenty or thirty gallons. Jesus said to them, 'Fill the jars with water.' And they filled them up to the brim. He said to them, 'Now draw some out, and take it to the chief steward.' So they took it. When the steward tasted the water that had become wine, and did not know where it came from (though the servants who had drawn the water knew), the steward called the bridegroom and said to him, 'Everyone serves the good wine first, and then the inferior wine after the guests have become drunk. But you have kept the good wine until now.' Jesus did this, the first of his signs, in Cana of Galilee, and revealed his glory; and his disciples believed in him.

JOHN 2:1–11

In high summer, you step outside on a fine day and witness nothing less than a party in full swing. The created order is in a season of lavish and wild celebration. The trees that once stretched their dark skeletal branches to a cold lacklustre sky are now laden with leaf and fruit. If you are a gardener, then you delight in the colourful life that has erupted from the quiet earth of your garden. In a summer breeze, brightly coloured flowers wave and flutter like bunting at a carnival. It is a deep human instinct to delight in this festival in creation, and as humans evolved, they took a leaf out of nature's book and invented their own summertimes of high celebration. They gathered to party together for the great celebrations of birth and the other rites of passage. One of the greatest of human festivals was the betrothal of two people in a ceremony that we now call a wedding.

In the days when Jesus walked this earth, weddings were common and greatly cherished, especially in those communities that were afflicted by poverty, because in the golden hours of celebration you could momentarily forget the daily life of hardship. There is some speculation about exactly how a Jewish wedding worked in first-century Galilee, but one thing is clear: it went on for several days and some have suggested that the partying went on for as long as the wine held out. It seems there were times when it ran out too soon, and this story of the wedding in Cana of Galilee is one such occasion.

I like to think of this story as seen through the eyes of the bride. She has longed for this magical celebration since she was a child. Now here she is in the moments she has anticipated for so long. She and her husband are dressed as royalty and never again will they be so exalted and honoured. The ceremony is behind them – the vows have been made under the wedding canopy, and the glass has been shattered under the foot of her young groom. The whole town seems to be here on this warm starlit night and a waxing moon gleams on the contented company. Children are running between the tables leaving a wake of parental rebukes. But nobody wants to be angry today, and even those who seldom have a civil word to say to others are succumbing to warm smiles in the flickering candlelight.

The bride coyly sips her cup of wine and gives her husband a tender and knowing glance. As she tips the cup, she notices it is empty and asks a servant to fill it from the large jug on the table. It is at that point she becomes aware that there is a problem with the wine. It appears to have run out. Anxiety becomes an unwelcome intruder into her happiness.

She watches the steward go over to Mary, a distant aunt whom she has always loved but hardly knows. She has often heard people speak about her eldest son whom she always called Yeshua, though many used the Greek version of his name, Jesus. He is a guest at her wedding and is standing by the great jars of water that people use for all the ritual washing that has to take place before meals. He is listening to an elderly lady whose arm movements suggest she is relating some magnificent drama that has featured somewhere in the long years of her life. The young bride's anxiety deepens as more people start asking about the wine.

She notices the steward and Mary now go over to Yeshua, who gestures to them to wait until his elderly companion completes her story. The young bride strains forward, but she cannot hear any words above the buzz of the crowd. The old lady shuffles away chuckling, and Yeshua turns to converse with his mother. Then Mary returns to her seat and the bride watches Yeshua speak to the steward, who looks puzzled but nods in agreement. He gives some instructions to a few servants, who curiously set about filling up the great jars with water from the nearby well. The bride starts to feel desperate – surely the steward will not give the guests lowly water on an occasion like this? She feels a mix of fear and shame as she sees the steward scooping the liquid out of the great jars and slopping it into the wine jugs. He pours himself a cup and the taste clearly surprises him, as he pulls back his head with a look of delight. The bride cannot comprehend why water from the well should please him so much. Her guests are not going to like being offered this.

The steward now brings the jug to her table and bows in front of her. 'We have wine,' he says calmly and she knows he has not. He pours the liquid into her goblet and to her astonishment she sees it is ruby red. 'It is his gift,' says the steward, and goes to fill other cups. The bride's hand shakes as she looks into the goblet. It is water, of course, and yet she detects the distinct and heady fragrance of wine. She draws the fluid to her lips and takes a tiny sip. The taste is heavenly. Is she imagining this? She takes another sip, followed by an undignified gulp. There can be no doubt about it: this is excellent wine. She has no idea how this can be, but she sits back in her chair in great relief, and beams at her husband and grasps his hand – there will be no shame or disgrace at their wedding. The magic has returned and if all those jars are full of this beautiful wine, the celebration can continue for several more days.

There may well have been some at that feast who spent the rest of the wedding trying to figure out how Jesus performed such an extraordinary trick. There would also be others who had seen something so special in this carpenter's son from Nazareth that they could see nothing particularly improbable about the miracle because, in their experience, so much of life seemed to turn special at his touch. For most of the guests, though, they were probably just delighted that someone had found such an abundance of excellent wine, and they were delighted that they could party for a good time yet.

There is something very heart-warming about the fact that in John's Gospel this story is the first recorded miracle of Jesus. Scholars will be quick to tell us the theological significance of this. But the most endearing feature of this story is Jesus' love of human celebration. Perhaps he simply could not bear for the party to end. Perhaps he was looking forward to when he would return as the true Bridegroom and be united to his people, his Bride, for whom he would die. For most people, their image of God is of a deity who is rather severe, tremendously serious and apt to disapprove of anything that looks too frivolous. The Cana story tells us that the God of the Gospels is anything but. When he chose to step into this world as a fellow human in the form of Jesus, he rolled up his divine sleeves, and mucked in with our broken world in its deepest sorrows and its highest celebrations. A wedding like that in Cana was a sign of human community flourishing as it was always meant to do.

Once, on another occasion, where people were running wild with excitement during a public festival, the sour-faced religious professionals tried to dampen the celebration with words of rebuke, to which Jesus replied, 'If you manage to silence them, then the rocks and stones will break out in cheers.'[50] He knew all about the irrepressible gift of celebration in this world he had fashioned.

Reflection

What is it you love about celebration?

Prayer

Dear God, when I am fortunate to be in a season of celebration, let me notice your presence, and let your transforming grace work its miracles in me.

Notes

1   William Shakespeare, *The Merchant of Venice*, Act 5 scene 1. Some may be familiar with these words from Vaughan Williams' *Serenade to Music*, which includes this quote.
2   Ecclesiastes 3:1.
3   John 3:1–36.
4   John 20:1.
5   2 Timothy 3:16.
6   Percy Bysshe Shelley, *Ode to Naples*, 1.i.
7   Most commentators agree that the author of this passage was writing to the people of Israel, who had been captured at the fall of Jerusalem in 587BC and were living as exiles in Babylon.
8   Walter Brueggemann, *Hopeful Imagination* (Fortress Press, 1986), p. 9. This is the title he gives to Part 1 of his book.
9   For examples of Jesus being called 'Son of David' see Matthew 15:22 and Matthew 20:30.
10 Leviticus 15:25–30.
11 Hebrews 13:2.
12 For more on *Fountain of Life Ministries*, see **www.flmhope.org**.
13 John 1:5.
14 'The Dark Night of the Soul' is the title given to a poem written by the 16th-century mystic John of the Cross.
15 Isaiah 45:3.
16 From John of the Cross' poem 'The Dark Night of the Soul'. The original is in Spanish and there are many English translations. This one is from **www.goodreads.com**.
17 Ruth 4:15.
18 Matthew 1:5.
19 A poem I wrote in 2003 for some friends who were suffering the severe grief of the loss of their son.
20 Exodus 20:13–17.
21 Matthew 3:7.
22 Matthew 23:27.
23 Matthew 12:24 – the Pharisees use the term 'Beelzebub', a contemporary name for the devil.
24 John 1:5.
25 1 Corinthians 15:6 tells us that Jesus appeared to more than 500 disciples in these days, and it is a reasonable guess to suppose that

one of those was Nicodemus, who cared so lovingly for Jesus after Calvary.

26 1 Kings 18:17.

27 The great contest on Mount Carmel is dramatically described in 1 Kings 18.

28 See I Kings 18:16–46 for this story.

29 Song of Songs 2:10–13.

30 Genesis 1:3–4.

31 Genesis 15:5.

32 Song of Songs 8:7.

33 Genesis 1:27.

34 Isaiah 18. Cush was Nubia or ancient Ethiopia, to the south of Egypt.

35 Isaiah 40—55. Chapters 1—39 are the Book of Judgement, and chapters 56—66 are the Book of Hope.

36 See for example Deuteronomy 15:15.

37 John 11:5.

38 Isaiah 52:7.

39 John 11:27.

40 See Ecclesiastes 3:11–14.

41 See Ecclesiastes 12:1–8.

42 Ecclesiastes 2:14.

43 Ecclesiastes 8:1.

44 Psalm 139:13–14.

45 These words are from the famous 40th chapter of Isaiah. When Mark tells us the story of John the Baptist, he also refers to it (Mark 1:3). The version used in my text is the one used by Martin Luther King in his famous 'I have a dream' address at the Lincoln Memorial in 1963.

46 Quoted in Maureen Stearns, *Conscious Courage: Turning everyday challenges into opportunities* (Enrichment Books, 2004), p. 99.

47 Matthew 6:25–34 (abridged).

48 Dean Allen, aged 40, interviewed by the *Daily Mirror*. He won a Lotto jackpot of £13 million in August 2000.

49 Philippians 4:12.

50 This story can be found in Luke 19:37–40.

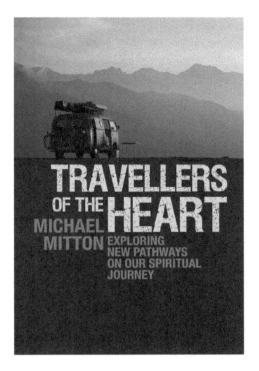

Michael Mitton explores how encompassing something of the breadth of Christian spirituality, from Charismatic to Catholic, via Celtic, can not only enrich our faith but strengthen the mission of the church: 'I have chosen to start with my own experience, not because I am any kind of expert but because the best tutors to me over the years have been those prepared to share with me their stories, their ups and downs of life, their struggles and discoveries. Often their experiences have been very different to my own, but as I listen to them, they help me reflect on what is taking place in me.'

Travellers of the Heart
Exploring new pathways on our spiritual journey
Michael Mitton
978 0 85746 221 3   £7.99

brfonline.org.uk

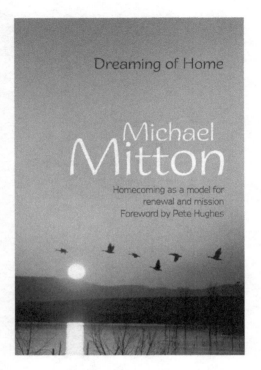

Dreaming of Home

Michael Mitton

Homecoming as a model for
renewal and mission
Foreword by Pete Hughes

Finding a sense of 'home', a special place of acceptance and belonging,
is a fundamental human longing. In this powerful and profound book,
Michael Mitton shows how it is in fact an essential part of both personal
development and spiritual renewal. Drawing on his own experience of the
'homecoming' journey, he considers how we can go about finding our true
home within God's eternal kingdom, how to identify the forces within us
that may hinder this search, and the importance of churches offering a
welcoming home to all.

Dreaming of Home
Homecoming as a model for renewal and mission
Michael Mitton
978 1 84101 877 5 £7.99

brfonline.org.uk